CONTENTS

Twentieth Century Slaves

High in the mountains of south-west China there live a race of people who, until recent times, were bound in slavery to their feudal masters.

A persistent rumour began spreading rapidly among people living high in the mountains of south-west China. It was whispered on frightened lips in the wattle huts where the most deprived people lived. And it was hissed through

It was whispered in the streets. The slaves were to be freed. But behind the rumour there lurked fear.

clenched lips in the pink adobe homes of the nobility. Everywhere groups of people had the same fear on their lips—death!

The word they should have shouted loud and clear was freedom, but this was a word without meaning for most of the people living at the top of a mountain range in China's Yunnan Province, sheltered by their high rocky range from the rest of China. This was the home of the Norsu people who, for centuries, had lived with a system of slavery which had persisted into the 20th century.

But things were changing in the rest of China. The Communists had come to power in 1948 and the system of serfdom was giving way to the principle of sharing the resources of the land equally among all the people.

Such a system could not allow slavery to continue. Working parties of helpers from other parts of China were coming to organise the liberation of the slaves, it was said. And it was then that the rumours began spreading.

The slave owners were afraid. They feared that their slaves would rise in a mass and take their revenge for their lives of forced labour. Not without reason were the slave owners worried, for they had beaten and ill-treated their slaves, possessed them completely and flogged them to death if they stole. It was not surprising that the owners feared the slaves' retribution.

The slaves were afraid. They thought that their owners would kill them rather than permit them to become free for the first time.

It was while this feeling of uncertainty was in the air that the people of the Yunnan Province, known as the Norsu, had their first visit from a European. The man who came to see them was Alan Winnington, a British journalist. Other Europeans had tried to penetrate this slave society high in the mountains, but none had succeeded. And those who succeeded in crossing the mountain barrier had never returned alive. One man's body was sent out in two pieces.

To this mysterious place, shown blank on most maps, Winnington went with two Chinese friends to learn about the slave society and to see the liberation of the slaves. For him it was a unique experience, for not only was he the first European to examine the

slave system here. but he was also probably the last because the system was in the process of being ended.

Winnington spoke to slaves and slave owners and built up a picture of the society which he describes in his book "The Slaves of the Cool Mountains" (Lawrence and Wishart Ltd.)

His journey to the Cool Mountains, where the Norsu live in a hot-house climate, took a week from the town of Li Chang at the foot of the mountains. It was a tough, rough journey up steep mountain trails on a horse that jibbed at the steep inclines and forced Winnington to cover much of the way on foot. Finally, he reached the chief town, Ningland, where he saw a muddy street lined with little stalls crowded with jostling people. This was the heart of the Norsu area and he was the first non-Chinese to see it.

For many weeks, Winnington stayed with the Norsu. He found a population of 56,000 people. Three thousand of these were tall, healthy and war-

like. They were the nobles—the slave owners. All the rest were either slaves or common bondsmen, who were little better than slaves. Fifty-three thousand people were living like cattle to enable three thousand to enjoy the lives of idleness. It seemed incredible

Most of them had begun their lives of slavery as tiny tots at the age of five or six. These were the house slaves, who began doing simple jobs like carrying water, and did harder jobs as they grew older. They stayed with their master until they died or were sold. Throughout their entire lives, they were allowed to possess nothing.

Slaves in the second of the two grades in which they were placed were a little better off. These were called separate slaves because they did not live in the master's house. They could have a simple wattle home, a small plot of land and even own slaves of their own.

Few of the slaves seemed to have thoughts of freedom, for generations of captivity had made them

Long conferences were necessary to help the people to change from slavery to freedom. But in the end, the transition was made peacefully and successfully.

accept their fate. Some had tried to escape, but most of them had been recaptured and flogged or killed publicly as a warning to the other slaves?

But could not a slave buy his freedom? Winnington asked a slave, who also owned two slaves of his own, why he did not sell his slaves to buy his liberty. This man explained that he and his wife were very expensive slaves. "Suppose I sold my two," he said. "I wouldn't even get enough to buy myself out, let alone my wife and children. We come from several generations of Norsu slaves."

The solution this man had adopted was to use his slaves to do his master's work so that the man was free to work for himself. "During the day they work for my master, and in the early morning and evening they work for me," he explained.

But the days of the slave-culture were numbered. With the establishment of Communism, big changes were taking place in the rest of China. Capitalism had been abolished, peasants were working on farming co-operatives, and men in factories were better off than the rich slave owners of Ninglang.

And it was inevitable that reforms should come to the Norsu as well. Six weeks of talks were needed to hammer out the best plan—a slow transition from captivity to freedom, made as painlessly as possible. Both classes, nobles and slaves, were treated fairly.

The nobles kept their rights as citizens, were given subsidies to maintain their living standards and some were paid salaries as local leaders. They also kept their homes, wealth and personal property, and were allowed to have more land than the other people.

The rest of the land was shared out among the slaves, according to the size of their families. Those with homes were free to return to them, and those without homes were encouraged to join with others to build homes and farm the land they were given.

And what of the feared uprising of the slaves against their masters and of the massacre of the slaves by the nobles? It never took place. There were a few cases of slave owners killing their slaves and of slaves killing their masters, but these were exceptional.

For the most part, the slaves were too docile to turn against their former lords. They had been born in captivity, were unable to think for themselves and were efficient only at obeying orders. Some celebrated their freedom by lolling about in idleness, until they were shown that they had to work if they wanted to live.

One of the first rural districts to complete the abolition of slavery was called Happy Stone Mountain. It has a good name for a good event—the ending of the last vestige of complete slavery in the modern world. Let us hope that there is now happiness everywhere among the people of the Cool Mountains.

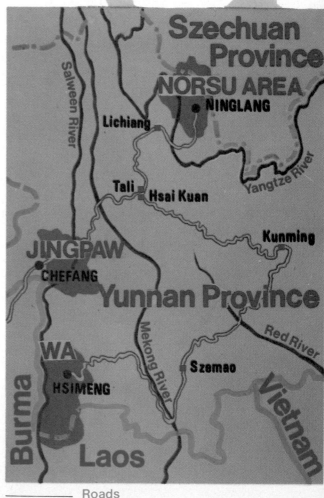

Roads

Undefined National Boundaries

4

Snake Dancers

A strange dance to encourage rain is performed by the Hopi Indians of north-east Arizona, U.S.A. The men dance in pairs, one holding a rattle-snake in his mouth while the other tickles the snake with a feather to prevent it biting. These Indians live in terraced houses made of sun-dried mud (above) called adobe.

In Search of Diamond River

When he heard of a river in Venezuela reputedly flowing with diamonds, an adventurer set off on a trek that was to bring him the friendship of an Indian youth, who shared his thrills and dangers in the quest for untold riches.

Gently, Sadio Garavini di Turno raised the sieve from the gravelly bed of the forest stream and shook it. As the water drained away, leaving a residue of stones, he sifted through them with trembling fingers. Excitedly, he pushed aside the chips of gravel and picked up one stone that his trained eyes told him was different from the others. It was a diamond weighing at least two carats. Putting this diamond carefully into a bag, he plunged his sieve into the gravel again and again, until four more diamonds appeared in the fine-meshed sieve.

As he straightened himself and rested from his labours, di Turno felt that he was at last on the trail of the fortune that had brought him to the hot steamy jungles of Venezuela in South America. It had been a chance remark from a friend in the city of Caracas that had sent him on the search for diamonds. After his farm had been destroyed by a hurricane, di Turno was sitting dejectedly in a cafe, wondering how to recover his losses, when this friend, an official of the Venezuelan government, told him of his visit to a tribe of Indians called the Taurepan.

"There's a river absolutely chock-a-block with diamonds," his friend had said. "You can imagine what would happen if the news got around. Why don't you have a shot at it?"

The river had no name, but the Indians called it Liparu. "It rises in Brazil and is a tributary of the Uia-paru," said the friend.

A few days later, armed with a sketch map of the area, di Turno set off on his quest for the river of diamonds. He flew to Cuidad Bolivar, stocked up with provisions for his expedition and went in a little chartered plane to Uriman, a small airport deep in Indian territory. There he engaged four men and a canoe to carry him deep into the jungle.

His journey through the jungle was an adventure in itself and it culminated in di Turno's arrival at a Taurepan village near the diamond river.

"Coming into this village was like being transported back into the Stone Age," he wrote. He saw a collection of huts made of wood and leaves. The people had wooden spears, stone vessels, woven straw baskets and flint axes. A river ran beside the village.

A dignified and impressive old man took di Turno into a hut to await the village headman, who was out hunting. Di Turno had a photograph of the headman, named Mundo, which he hoped would serve as an introduction. Mundo had been taught some Spanish by di Turno's friend, for whom he had acted as a guide, so it would be possible for di Turno, who also spoke Spanish, to converse with him.

Eventually, Mundo, a tall man with thick-set features, returned from his hunting trip and came across to di Turno, demanding, "Why you come this place?"

Mundo was tough, suspicious and strong-willed, and di Turno quickly pointed out that he had not come to make trouble. "This territory contains stones that are of much interest to white people," said di Turno, referring to the diamonds he was seeking.

After further talk, Mundo allowed di Turno to stay, although his hostility had not entirely gone. But later, after di Turno had been able to use the medicine he carried to save a sick Indian, opposition to him evaporated and he was allowed to stay, living in the village as one of the inhabitants.

The youth whose disease he conquered was named Antu—he was Mundo's nephew—and a strong friendship grew between the lad and di Turno. And it was Antu who accompanied di Turno on his first exploratory expedition to find the diamonds. While he was on a later expedition with Antu and two others from the village, di Turno found more of the precious stones and realised that the river in which he discovered them was being fed from a stream that flowed from inside a mountain.

The diamonds were being carried into the river from the sides

and bed of the rock-tunnel through which the water flowed. If he could discover this source, di Turno realised that he would find an Aladdin's cave filled with wealth beyond all imagination.

Various openings in the mountain sides were explored, but they all proved impenetrable. The sound of a waterfall within the mountain tantalised di Turno and made his thwarted efforts all the more frustrating.

"No one had penetrated to the pool in the centre of the mountain," he wrote in his book "Diamond River" (Hamish Hamilton Ltd.) "By now it must be some sort of vast treasure chest. The diamond fever was upon me again and I could hardly wait to get my hands on the stuff."

After several days of failure, exhausted by crawling along dozens of tunnels, he found an opening high up the mountain-side from which the sound of water was clearly audible.

He knotted two lengths of liana rope together, entwined one end around a palm tree, and lowered himself into the hole. Antu paid out the rope cautiously as di Turno descended. After about thirty feet, he touched the ground.

After crawling along a narrow passage, di Turno found himself in a large grotto in which was another tunnel from which came the sound of rushing water. By edging his way on his hands and knees along this, di Turno discovered a vast cavern filled with weird echoes from the boom of the rushing water. The water fell into a pool some ten yards across.

This was enough for the first visit. Di Turno crawled out of the mountain and returned the next day with Antu bringing a

Diamond after diamond appeared in the fine-meshed sieve, and di Turno felt that at last he was on the trail of the fortune that had brought him to the jungles of Venezuela.

bucket, a shovel handle and a crowbar. The pair stood in the icy subterranean pool and di Turno examined the pool's bottom which formed a single, hard, compact diamond-bearing formation.

They banged away at the bottom with the crowbar and filled the bucket with rock chips, which were hauled up by their companions. After five bucketfuls had been sent to the surface, the men returned and washed the stones to see what they had collected.

They found three two-carat diamonds, about ten small gold nuggets, a score of small diamonds and a sizable quantity of gold dust. For several days more, they worked in this fashion, and their stock of gold and diamonds rose visibly.

After four months of prospecting, di Turno and his companions returned to the Indian village. From there di Turno went by canoe to Caracas. Then he flew to Cuidad Bolivar and obtained five claims from the government each claim being 999 acres and situated on the Brazilian frontier between Rio Blanco and Uaiparu.

"Thus I found myself the owner of a large territory which I knew to be rich in gold and diamonds. I had become a man without financial worries," wrote di Turno in his book.

Sometime later, he set up a mining camp and arranged for the area's riches to be recovered. He had achieved what he had set out to do. He had found the fabulous riches that abounded in the Diamond River deep in the heart of Venezuela, where the people lived their simple, primitive lives.

If the Indian's way of life was disturbed by the miners and their activities, it was a temporary disturbance and in due course, when the mining was completed, tranquility returned to the village near the river that flowed with diamonds.

Antu paid out the rope cautiously as di Turno descended in search of an underground grotto and the wealth of diamonds he was sure it contained.

Adventurer of the Airways

Flying was an adventure in the years just after the First World War when intrepid young airman were blazing the trails that the big airlines were later to follow. Among the pioneers of the air was Alan Cobham who braved dangers in his quest for progress.

A little aeroplane buzzed through the sky like a busy wasp. In the cockpit sat Alan Cobham, a pioneer pilot who had first flown during the First World War and had since become famous as an airborne explorer. Already he had flown from England to Cape Town in South Africa and back, and to India and back.

But now he was engaged on one of the most adventurous flights of his career—a flight from England to Australia and back in a biplane fitted with floats to enable it to land on rivers and in harbours, for this was 1926 and there were very few aerodromes on which a conventional plane could land.

He had left England in June. It was now July and he was flying over Arabia towards the head of the Persian Gulf, having no inkling of the danger which lay ahead. All around him was a thick cloud of brown dust which was as blinding as a dense fog. And for Cobham this was a serious handicap, for he had no radio or radar to guide him, and he was navigating with a map, a compass and by the aid of visible landmarks.

Until the dust storm arrived,

he had been following the coastline of a swamp, but this, being brown, was now thoroughly blotted out by the brown dust.

Cobham flew down to a height of forty feet, wiping the brown dust from his goggles in an effort to see the coastline, for the dust was thinner at the lower altitude.

Sitting in a cabin behind him was Cobham's mechanic, Mr. A. B. Elliott, who shared Cobham's delight when they swooped out of the dust and saw the landmark they had been seeking.

They were happy and relieved, but to a man hunting on the edge of the swamp they were a spectacle of terror. He had never seen an aeroplane before, probably never even heard of one. All that he knew was that a throbbing metal monster had suddenly materialised as the dust storm subsided. He raised the rifle he was carrying, took aim and fired.

An explosion shook the little plane. Cobham thought that one of their rocket-pistol cartridges had exploded, and he shouted to Elliott to ask what had happened. Elliott replied that a petrol pipe had burst and that he was bleeding severely from a wound in his arm. Cobham turned round and saw that Elliott was as pale as a ghost and obviously severely wounded. Neither of them suspected that they had been fired at from the ground.

Cobham was in a dilemma. Would it be better to land and try to attend to Elliott's wound or should he fly nearly a hundred miles to the town of Basra in Iraq where there was a hospital? He decided to head for Basra, flying over strange country that he could hardly see in intense heat. In forty minutes, he had got to Basra. On the crowded river, there seemed to be no place to land. But he spotted a small mud bank and somehow brought down the machine to a perfect landing.

Switching off the engine, Cobham clambered into the cabin to find Elliott white and weak from loss of blood. An improvised stretcher was made with the help of local people and Elliott was taken to hospital, where it was

found that his injuries had been caused by a bullet which had broken an arm and passed through his left lung. After losing so much blood, Elliott had little chance of survival, and he died the next day.

The shock to Cobham was so great that he at first wanted to call off the flight. Then the local R.A.F. station offered to lend him a mechanic in the form of Sergeant A. H. Ward, and Cobham decided to continue. Little more than a week later, he and his new companion set off again for Australia.

Flying in stages of 400 or 500

Sir Alan Cobham, whose flight to Australia and back in 1926 made history.

miles, they made their way southwards in a series of hops. Fuel supplies had been arranged before the flight had begun, for a great deal of preliminary organisation was necessary in the days when commercial flights were in their infancy. The purpose of Cobham's flight was to prove that an air route to Australia could be flown by the aeroplanes of his day so that a commercial service could be organised in the future.

They made stops on the shores of the Indian Ocean, and then flew for nearly 2,000 miles across

Northern India. This part of the journey was done in four stages and involved landing on rivers where space was restricted and strong currents were a menace.

Eventually, they reached the harbour of Darwin in Australia in August. Lying in the harbour was an Australian naval ship, whose crew removed the plane's floats and put an undercarriage in their place. Cobham then flew across the Australian continent to Melbourne and a victorious welcome by the people.

A fortnight later, he took off again, heading for home in 500 mile hops, eventually reaching London on 1st October, 1926 where thousands of cheering people saw him land on the River Thames.

In 320 flying hours he had covered 28,000 miles in his DH50 biplane powered by an Armstrong-Siddeley Jaguar engine. A few days later, he was made a Knight Commander of the British Empire which provided official recognition of his courage as a flying pioneer.

But this was not the end of Cobham's exploits as a flyer. He led a flying boat expedition around the African continent, and organised flying displays in Britain during the 1930s. His efforts and those of the other pioneers led to commercial air routes gradually creeping around the world. They began modestly with weekly air mail services, gradually extending to the carriage of passengers. Links with India, Cairo, Delhi, Cape Town and Singapore were started.

Eventually, in 1935, the first passenger service to Australia was begun, and by 1938, when this had become an established route, people could fly to Darwin in Northern Australia in seven days and to Brisbane on the other side of the continent in nine days. Today, fast jets can whisk you to Darwin in about 30 hours and on to Brisbane in another five.

And all this is due, in no small measure, to the courage of a flyer in a small plane braving the unknown fifty years ago to blaze a trail in the skies for the big jets of today to follow.

As the throbbing, metal monster suddenly materialised out of a dust storm, the frightened tribesman raised his rifle, took aim and fired.

11

THE FROZEN PARADISE

It was the coldest place on Earth - the south geomagnetic pole - but to Bob Thomson and his team who had trekked halfway across Antarctica to reach it, the snow-banked station they found there was a haven amid the icy wastes.

"C'mon you guys, the plane's here! It's been flying over us for ages."

Danny Foster flung open the door of a caravan, letting the subzero wind of the Antarctic howl in. He yelled his message at the sleepy inhabitants, and was gone. As the four men in the caravan sprang out of their bunks, a quickening roar indicated that the plane was making another pass overhead.

Dazzling bright sunshine reflected off the icy plateau as the men hurried from their caravan and stared at the black spot in the sky.

To the pilot, they must have made a forlorn sight Their expedition of one Weasel and two Caterpillar tractors towing sledges with all their supplies, and a caravan used for their sleeping quarters, was a strange spectacle in the middle of hundreds of miles of unbroken snow and ice. The destination of this Australian National Antarctic Research Expedition was a Russian station named Vostok at the south geomagnetic pole—the coldest place on earth.

It was manned by three Australians and one American who were led by a New Zealander, Bob Thomson, a rugged veteran of previous Antarctic expeditions. For 572 miles, the party had crawled through the ice in sub-zero temperatures from their base at Wilkes station on the coast of East Antarctica. They were now over halfway to Vostok. But their fuel had almost run out.

They could return to their base, because they had laid down fuel dumps during their traverse. But they could not go on to their target—Vostok—without more diesel oil for the tractors. And that was the object of their excitement at this point for the plane was an American one bringing their fuel.

The temperature of 100 degrees below freezing hit Bob Thomson like a hammer, as hurriedly dressed with too few clothes to protect him from the blistering cold, he climbed into a tractor and switched on its radio to contact the pilot. But its batteries were frozen and it refused to work.

Scrambling into another tractor, Bob switched its radio on. Amazingly this showed signs of life and he pounded a message in morse to the pilot.

"Where is your drop zone?" radioed the pilot.

"West of caravans and vehicles," Bob keyed clumsily the cold brass of the morse key burning his bare fingers.

The plane, a Globemaster, approached rapidly and when it was nearly overhead, two dark objects fell away from its tail. The plan was for the drums of oil to be lowered gently by parachute. But in this case the parachutes failed to open, and the oil drums crunched on the surface and disappeared in a great spray of broken ice and powdery snow.

Back came the plane. More runs were made over the dropping zone and eight sets of bundles were dropped by parachutes which billowed as they neared the surface

Bob tapped out a message of

"The plane's here," yelled Danny Foster, arousing the others of his party to the fact that a much-needed supply of fuel was about to be dropped by parachute.

thanks with his frozen fingers. "Total 31 drums received in good order. Four lost first pallet. Many thanks for your help. Wish you good flight back to McMurdo."

McMurdo was the base from which the plane had flown, a thousand miles away. To bring that oil had involved the pilot in a round trip of some 2,000 miles and ten hours of flying.

When it was over, Bob looked at his frost-bitten fingers and said, "What a hectic time that was. But most successful, so we should be okay now and can push on towards Vostok."

The oil drums were dragged on sledges to the vehicles and the oil pumped into empty fuel tanks.

By late evening of the next day, after they had been delayed by a blizzard, the party set off for Vostok, 317 miles away across territory which no man had crossed before, for all previous traverses had been by air.

The object of going overland was to enable one of their party, a geophysicist, to make seismic surveys to discover the thickness of the ice, for their destination was at an extremely high altitude 11,500 ft. above sea level—and for meteorological work to be undertaken as well.

Bob Thomson and Danny Foster, the meteorologist, led the way in one tractor, with the rest of the party following in the other vehicles. At a speed of a few miles an hour—30 miles an hour, when they could make it, seemed fast—the party crept towards Vostok. They crunched over hard ice, sank into valleys, crawled over peaks and made repairs to their tractors' metal tracks with the ice forming on their faces and their fingers suffering from contact with the cold metal. For some work had to be done with the bare hands, and intensely cold metal burns as badly as if it were red hot.

Finally, when they were ten miles from Vostok, with nothing in sight, Thomson began to have doubts about the efficiency of his navigation. "Finding their base was worse than trying to find a small boat on a great ocean," he wrote in his book, "The Coldest Place on Earth". He added, "And what would we be looking for anyway? Any huts that may have existed could by now be covered by snow. If so, we had nothing to look for, nothing to find."

However, they decided to push on and were rewarded by seeing a black mast on the horizon and then huts and many other vertical rods which could be aerial masts.

"Boy oh boy, we've made it," cried Bob. He fired a Very pistol to pass the good news to the others trailing far behind, Nev Collins, "Pancho" Evans, Don Walker and Alastair Battye.

As they travelled, the black dots grew into large tracked Russian vehicles, caravans and sledges and parts of huts and equipment just showing above the snow.

"I jumped out on to the surface," wrote Bob Thomson. "This was a little mean to Danny, perhaps, but I did so want to be the first person, other than a Russian, to set foot at Vostok, the south geomagnetic pole, the Pole of Cold, the coldest place on Earth."

Unfortunately, there was nobody at home to welcome them.

Bob Thomson jumped out on to the ice when the tractor stopped, anxious to be the first member of the expedition to set foot on the coldest place on Earth.

The base was unmanned, although the Russians were due to occupy it a month or so later.

However, the Australian party made themselves at home on the base for a few days while they rested before making their return journey. They recorded a temperature of minus 121.7 degrees, five degrees above the coldest temperature recorded on Earth two years previously.

They got the Russian heaters working, warmed up the huts, had a bath and ate some food the Russians had left and even watched a long evening of films including a silent Charlie Chaplin movie and a Russian version of "Pygmalion". And all this in the midst of a vast ocean of ice.

A few days later they set off for home leaving a note of thanks

Relief from their awesome traverse was provided at a deserted Russian station where they watched a long evening of films, including an old Charlie Chaplin movie.

to the Russians for the use of the base—they had previously obtained permission from the Russians to do so—and began the traverse back to their base at Wilkes.

After an arduous journey, during which they survived some of the worst weather of the whole traverse, they returned to their base amid a welter of congratulatory telegrams from all over the world. A party from Wilkes came out in tractors to meet them and escort them home in style.

They had survived many bliz-

zards and whiteouts (in which nothing can be seen but fine driving snow) to travel the 900 miles to Vostok and back in the coldest temperatures man has ever known. For 120 days they had been pioneers in the unknown. The date of their arrival at Vostok was 18th November, 1962.

A few years later, in 1969, Bob Thomson flew to Vostok to be an honoured guest of the Russians, spent two hours with them, and flew back to McMurdo base 810 miles away in two-and-a-half hours.

"This time, everything's been so easy," he thought, "unlike the time when Vostok had been a godsend providing simple shelter and a few amenities after a trek of some hundreds of miles over the bleak, lonely wastes of Antarctica."

A STONE AGE WONDER IN THE ORKNEYS

A Stone Age village, perfectly preserved for centuries beneath many feet of sand, was discovered when archaeologists began their explorations of a storm-swept island in the Orkneys.

Ancient pieces of bone, each showing traces of paint that was probably thousands of years old, lay in the sand on the shore of a storm-swept bay in the Orkneys, a group of islands to the north of Scotland.

Archaeologists, digging in the dunes here—the Bay of Skaill on the Atlantic coast of the biggest island in the group—had found them. Their curiosity had at first been aroused when strange groups of large stones were uncovered when a severe storm had washed away the peaks from the great dunes in which they were buried. And they wanted to know what else lay beneath the surface.

As they scooped away the sand, the men saw the painted pieces of bone seemingly forming a trail away from the stones they were uncovering. And in them they read the story of a tragedy that must have happened in the times of pre-history. For the clues they discovered took them back about 4,000 years. Then the Orkneys, isolated from the rest of Britain among the wild seas to the north of Scotland, retained a pocket of Stone Age culture after the rest of Britain had entered the Bronze Age.

What the archaeologists were finding under the sand was a village in which everything was made of stone—houses, furniture and tools—or of bone obtained from animals. Here under the

A general view of the Stone Age settlement in the Orkneys as it appears today. The tops of the walls have been turfed so that the work of the original builders can be preserved.

sand was a community of eight stone houses, with paved alleys leading to each and also to a workshop, where the men had prepared the skins to be made into clothes and had shaped clay into crockery and cooking pots. And here, also, worked the craftsmen who painted small pieces of bone to make strings of beads for the young women of the village to wear.

One day, while she was wearing her beads a young woman of the village appears to have been startled by a fierce storm that raged in the bay, piling up sand against the stone homes. To escape from the tempest, she and her people fled. As she ran, the

girl's beads must have caught on the stone post of her doorway, breaking the strand. While she raced for safety, the girl's beads fell to the ground one by one, leaving a poignant trail of terror that lay in the sand for thousands of years as mute testimony to a prehistoric tragedy.

If the villagers returned to their home after the storm, they would have seen a sad sight. The entire village of houses, alleys and workshop was completely buried by an enormous mountain of sand, swept over it by the powerful storm.

Nothing remained to show that a busy community had once lived here. History might have closed

When a storm threatened to engulf their village, the people raced for safety. One girl's necklace broke, leaving a trail of beads for archaeologists, centuries later, to follow.

the story of the village at this point had not another great storm in 1851 rushed in from the North Sea and torn away some of the sand from the Stone Age settlement. Another storm in 1926 cleared away more sand. Sufficient of the village was now visible to persuade the archaeologists that here was a find worth investigating.

After years of painstaking work, they were given the reward for

their labours. Before their eyes lay the most perfect Stone Age village in Europe, preserved in all its detail by the sand which had laid over it for centuries. It was an archaeologists' dream come true, a thing unique in the annals of British pre-historic science. And among the souvenirs of a past civilisation were the young woman's beads trailed in the sand where they had fallen when she ran for her life all those ages ago.

Skara Brae is the name of the village, and it lies in the Bay of Skaill flanked by hills rising to lofty cliffs. It contains eight one-roomed houses, each with a low, narrow doorway through which the occupants had to crawl into their home. Every house was made of stones laid one upon the other without mortar. Their roofs, which no longer remain, are thought to have been made of whalebone rafters supporting slates or thatch, for a whalebone was found that could have been a roof support.

To lock up their homes at night, the villagers heaved a huge stone across the doorway and kept it in place with a stone bar lodged in sockets in the wall. Once inside, they were cosy and safe from the strong winds which blew in the bay. They sat on stone benches, ate limpets stored in salt water in a stone tank, or enjoyed a supper of beef or mutton, for they kept herds of cattle and sheep. Sometimes, the men would go to bed chewing a large beef or mutton bone, gnawing it clean before they dropped off to sleep. Some

of their bedplaces were cluttered with such bones.

Their beds were nothing but stone boxes packed with heather, and in this heather the women put their beads when they slept, along with pots of red, yellow and white paint which they used to make themselves look smart in the mornings.

Let into the wall above the beds was an alcove, where the housewife could put her bracelets and pendants made in the village workshop. And the children had their own little stone-walled beds

Visitors can still see the Stone Age cupboards (like the one in the back of this picture) where the housewife could keep her bracelets and pendants and other personal adornments.

in which they could curl up for the night on their mattresses of heather.

Cooking was done on peat in an open hearth in the centre of the room. On rare occasions, when the hunters had been exceptionally successful, red deer, wild boar, seal or whale were cooked on this.

Living must have been hard in the Orkneys in these times for, apart from the incessant hunting for food, rival warlike tribes were prowling the islands. To protect themselves from these, the villagers turned their community into a fortress. All the alleys linking the houses were roofed with slabs of stone or slate. And over these, and also over the houses, were banked heaps of sand, peat-ash and dung so that the entire village looked like one enormous mound with nothing visible except the opening of the tunnels which led to the alleys. It became in reality,

a subterranean village, easily covered by storm-swept sand and thus an ideal place for preservation through the centuries.

So low and narrow were the tunnels that led to the homes that they were easily defended against invaders. Probably, the people would have planned their defences and organised their hunting expeditions in the communal work shop, which seems to have been a central meeting place. Axe heads and knives of stone, and tools and pins of bone were found here. They also made the trinkets for their womenfolk, for nearly a thousand finished beads were found here, and unfinished ones lay scattered on the floor.

From such evidence, we can build up a picture of these people, although we know very little about

The villagers sat on stone benches, ate limpets stored in salt water, or enjoyed a supper of beef or mutton.

their origin. The skull shape of their skeletons—three were found in the village—suggests that they were part of a mixed population of long skulled folk (or Mediterraneans) and round-headed people (or Alpines). But we do know that they represented a local Stone Age flourishing while the rest of Europe had entered the Bronze Age or even the Iron Age.

Even this knowledge would have been denied to us but for the storms which buried the village and then uncovered it centuries later so that the people of today can look with wonder and awe at an imperishable mystery from the past.

The stone framework of a couch-bed in one of the huts in the stone age settlement.

WEALTH BEYOND THE MOUNTAINS

Beyond the 52nd parallel in British Columbia lay an awesome chunk of mountain, swamp, river and valley. Amid it were grasslands reaching as far as the eye could see.

An empire of grassy plains lay ahead of the two men, but before they could reach them they had to negotiate mountain trails and dangerous bogs.

Panhandle Phillips looked up sheepishly as the door of the bunkhouse opened and Richmond Hobson walked in. "Sit down, and I'll show ya something," said Panhandle.

He was squatting in the middle of the floor of the bunkhouse at a ranch in Wyoming, U.S.A., where the two men were ranch hands. Rich, as Richmond was called by his friends, had just come back from a neighbouring ranch. It was late at night and he was surprised to see Panhandle with maps and papers all around him.

Rich peered through the yellow light of the oil lamp as Panhandle jabbed his finger at a large sheet about four feet square. "See this map," said Panhandle. "Look at those little dotted lines ending with arrows."

There was practically nothing on the sheet, but at one corner a dark, winding line had "Blackwater River" printed along it.

"What's the idea?" said Rich. "Is this a map of hidden treasure or a gold mine?"

"Yes," said Pan. "A gold mine."

But the gold Pan was talking about was not the gleaming metal that men have died for in the far north of Canada, but grass. The map was of a then uncharted part of British Columbia, beyond the Itcha Mountains, where only scattered bands of Indians lived and no white man had explored. "There's reports of a grass country in there some place that reaches as far as the eye can see," said Pan. "Land—lots of it—just waiting for hungry cows, and some buckaroos that can ride and have guts enough to go there."

Cattlemen were creeping their herds back further in this frontier ranch country all the time, but none had gone beyond the Itcha Mountains. "They don't know what's over the other side," said Pan. "Maps don't show. Ya see, Rich, I sent to the B.C. government for maps and any pointers they got on the country."

Rich turned up the lamp wick and the room brightened. "When are we leaving?" he said.

And that is how it began, a big adventure by two men to explore the unknown land beyond the mountains and establish an enormous cattle ranch there. The year was 1934 and their objective was an awesome, 250,000 square mile chunk of mountain, swamp, river and valley north of the 52nd parallel.

A few weeks after their late night discussion, the two cowboys set off in a van and rattled across the Canadian frontier. They had been given the encouragement of a big rancher in Wyoming who had promised to finance them in setting up a frontier cattle company "if it's really big and you think it's a cattle company proposition."

During the journey north, the van was abandoned and, by trading with friendly ranchers, the two men obtained a horse apiece and, with the goodwill of many friends they had made on the way, they found themselves on the edge of the unexplored territory. They had lived in cabins and tents in temperatures far below freezing on this arduous trip, but now they were on the verge of their great discovery.

They saw it when they climbed a giant peak of the Algak Range and looked through binoculars and saw a wide, open sweep of grass land—an empire of grass that could be surveyed and bought for a few dollars an acre from the B.C. government.

But it was still miles away and to reach it they had to negotiate mountain trails and dangerous bogs. Steadily,

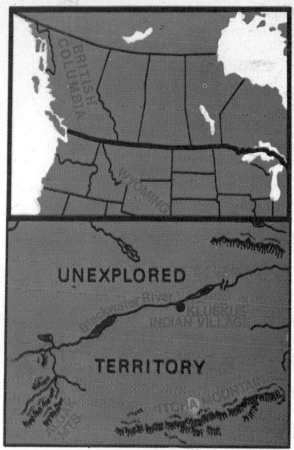

Rich Hobson and Panhandle Phillips trekked from Wyoming to British Columbia (top map) to enter unexplored territory beyond the Itcha Mountains where they hoped to find rich grasslands that would make them cattle kings.

they plunged northwards. plagued by mosquitoes and dysentery until they reached their destination, a gigantic hay meadow that dipped in a great low curve into an empty horizon.

They set up their camp and were beginning to take stock of the land, when they heard the sound of Indian drums. "Tum tum tum—boom, tum tum tum—boom," they throbbed through the day and the night. "Ulgatcho Indians," Pan said. "We must be prepared to meet them."

Pan thought that the Indians would have to be handled with kid gloves, that they would resent the white men moving into their country and that they would resort to any method short of murder to get them to move back to the white man's land on the other side of the mountains.

"Maybe they'll need some bluffin', maybe a little bit of scarin'—and then there's got to be some kind of a truce made with 'em," said Panhandle.

The next day they heard horse's hoofs padding on the pine needles at the back of their tent. Rich looked up and saw two Indians slipping off their short-legged horses.

Pan told Rich to make some coffee. He was wearing a Smith and Wesson 44 in a holster and barked at one of the Indians whose hand was on the butt of a small pearl-handled revolver, "Take your hand off that gun or you're gonna get killed."

The Indian obeyed, and Pan handed each of them a cup of coffee. For a while, the Indians drank in silence. They had jet black hair, slanting eyes and narrow, bony faces. Finally, one of them said, "White man, you go— this country belong Ulgatcho Indian." This was the ultimatum Pan and Rich had been expecting. Pan snatched the Indian's gun from its holster, flung a can of milk at the river and with his own Smith and Wesson sent shots singing after it that bounced the can and finally sank it.

"Big gun much better," said Pan, handing the Indian back his gun.

The man's eyes were popping, and the other Indian shook his fist at Rich and said, "Me best fight man Ulgatcho. I show you. Then you go."

Rich had been a sparring partner for professional boxers before he had become a cowboy, and he had some twelve ounce practice gloves which he used for sparring with Panhandle.

These were produced, tied on and the fight began. The Indian fought furiously, and Rich ducked, side-stepped and lunged. A haymaker put him in a daze.

But he recovered, avoided the Indian's club-like swings and stopped a head-on charge with his whole weight behind a straight left which landed on the Indian's forehead. He followed it with a right to the jaw.

The Indian crashed to the ground and lay still.

"Wowie," said Pan.

When the Indians rode away that night, they carried presents from the cowboys of an old opera hat, an old, white evening scarf, packaged soup, beef cubes and tea. These were from Rich. Pan gave them a pair of silk stockings (for one of their wives), some silver mounted spurs and an old car licence, as well as his assurance that the white men would not interfere with the Indians' beaver and other fur.

And so a truce was made, and the cowboys were free to establish their claim to their new territory. In 1937, this was accomplished. Financial backing was received and, in due course, an enormous herd of cattle and horses was being trailed to their new cattle range, which extended over four million acres.

They had crossed the last great cattle frontier in the North American continent, a frontier as tough and as wild as the West of the old days, between the Rockies and the Pacific ocean. And they brought prosperity to a lonely land of pine forests, loon-haunted lakes, timber wolves, beavers and moose. A land where grass prairies and yellow-green meadows glide between the mountain ranges that reach up to the sky.

To show the Indians that he was a marksman to be reckoned with, [he] flung a can at the river and sent shots singing after it.

OUR WORLD QUIZ

**Now that you have read the world section of this book,
see how many of the questions you can answer in the quiz
below. The answers are at the back of the book.**

1. What is the name of the race of Indians of north-east Arizona who perform a dance with a snake to encourage rain?

2. In what province of China did slavery persist into modern times and what political movement brought this to an end?

3. It was feared that, when the slaves were freed, they would rise against their former owners and massacre them. Did this happen?

4. Which pioneer pilot flew from England to Australia and back in 1926 in 320 flying hours? How many miles did he cover?

5. Was the aircraft used on the flight to Australia a monoplane, a biplane or a triplane?

6. What was the name of the mountains beyond which Rich Hobson and "Panhandle" Phillips found a vast area of rich grasslands in British Columbia?

7. After a show of strength, they made peace with the Indians they found there. To what tribe did these Indians belong?

8. Sadio Garavini di Turno found a river in Venezuela flowing with riches. What form did this wealth take?

9. He stayed with a tribe of Indians and was helped by the headman and his nephew. What were the names of the tribe and the two men?

10. How many claims did di Turno obtain from the government and what was the size of each claim?

11. What is the official name of the part of Antarctica known as the coldest place on Earth, to which an Australian expedition travelled?

12. Who was the leader of this expedition and what nationality was he?

13. At their destination, the expedition found a disused station at which they stayed. Which country had set up this station?

14. A perfectly preserved Stone Age village was found in a lonely part of Britain. Can you name this area?

15. Fragments of bone revealed a flight for safety made by a woman when a storm threatened the village. What are these pieces of bone thought to have come from?

16. In what year did a great storm wash away the sand covering the village and encourage archaeologists to complete its excavation?

17. Can you remember the name of the village? In what bay is it and how many dwellings does it contain?

18. Cooking was done on an open hearth in the centre of the room. What fuel was used on this?

19. What were the Norsu people and what happened to them after the Communists came to power in China?

20. What was the name of Alan Cobham's mechanic who was killed by a rifle shot on their outward journey from Britain?

Out Of This World

Two of the most significant events in the still short history of space flight occurred within two years of each other. The greatest scientific and technical task ever undertaken by Man came to its climax at 0256 hours GMT on Monday, 20th July, 1969 when Neil Armstrong climbed slowly down the ladder of his space craft and, planted his boot on the surface of another body in the heavens.

The second historic event occurred on 7th June, 1971, when three Russian cosmonauts, Georgi Dobrovolski,

Vladislav Volkov and Victor Patsayev, moved from their Soyuz 11 craft into Salyput, the world's first space station which had been sent into orbit ahead of them.

They set up house in the space station and for nearly 23 days and nights they ate, drank, slept and carried out much scientific work. In short they lived and worked in space for more than three weeks.

Now, let us go back to the beginning and then into the future of man's explorations in space.

25

SPUTNIK I. The world's first artificial satellite put into orbit by Russia on 4th October, 1957. It was a 23 inches diameter sphere weighing 184 lbs.

LAIKA. The first living creature to go into space was the Russian dog, "Laika", on 3rd November, 1957. She remained alive in her container for a week.

EXPLORER I. (left). The first American artificial satellite to go into orbit. Launched by Jupiter C rocket on 31st January, 1958. It was about six feet long (as shown) and carried 30 pounds of scientific instruments. The early explorer satellites were restricted in size and weight by the power of the available launch rockets. This was really the starting point in America's vast and ambitious space programme which resulted in men landing upon the Moon and our knowledge of the complexities of space travel being extended.

LUNA III. Launched on 4th October, 1959, this space craft was the first to fly round the Moon. It provided the first photographs of the far hitherto unseen side of the Moon. Cameras on the craft took these as it flew past, within 4,373 miles of the Moon. The timing was arranged so that the Sun's angle would show up the features of the moon's surface as clearly as possible. These photographs were sent back to Earth by radio and published in newspapers and magazines throughout the world, as well as being shown on television.

TIROS (left). The first meteorological satellite, launched on 1st April, 1960. Orbiting the Earth about once every 100 minutes, it carried cameras which took very clear pictures of the cloud formations 450 miles up. Two of these are shown on the right. From the weather patterns, meteorologists were able to improve their forecasts.

BELKA (left) and Strelka returned safely after a space flight in Sputnik 5, in August, 1960, the first living creatures to do so.

YURI GAGARIN (above) became the first man in space when he lifted off from the Baikonur Cosomodrome at 0907 hours, Moscow time, on 12th April, 1961, in his Vostok capsule.

ECHO I. Launched in August, 1960, this was the first passive communications satellite designed to reflect or "bounce" signals from one Earth station to another without amplifying them electronically.

VOSTOK. On the right is the rocket which put Gagarin and his capsule in orbit.

These diagrams show the Vostok capsule's re-entry sequence. As the retro-rocket was fired, the retro-pack was released and the clean, spherical capsule began its re-entry. The cosmonaut could (as shown right) remain in the capsule or parachute down.

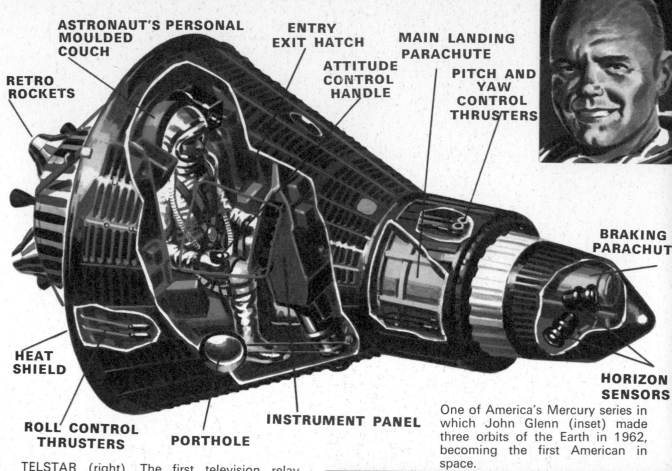

ASTRONAUT'S PERSONAL MOULDED COUCH

ENTRY EXIT HATCH

MAIN LANDING PARACHUTE

RETRO ROCKETS

ATTITUDE CONTROL HANDLE

PITCH AND YAW CONTROL THRUSTERS

BRAKING PARACHUT

HEAT SHIELD

HORIZON SENSORS

ROLL CONTROL THRUSTERS

PORTHOLE

INSTRUMENT PANEL

One of America's Mercury series in which John Glenn (inset) made three orbits of the Earth in 1962, becoming the first American in space.

TELSTAR (right). The first television relay satellite. It made history on 11th July, 1962, when the first picture was transmitted via Telstar from Andover, Maine, U.S.A., to Europe. Later experiments enabled Americans and Europeans to see "live" pictures of events in each other's countries as they were happening. Regular links between Britain and America are now frequent, thanks to these early experiments.

VALENTINA TERESHKOVA (left) was the first and, so far, only woman in space. On 16th June, 1963, she was launched in Vostok 6 and orbited in company with Valery Bykovsky who had already been in orbit for two days in Vostok 5, code-named Hawk.

VOSTOK 6 (left) in which Valetina Tereshkova became the first woman in space.

RANGER 7 (below) sped toward the Moon in July, 1964 taking pictures until it crashed on the surface.

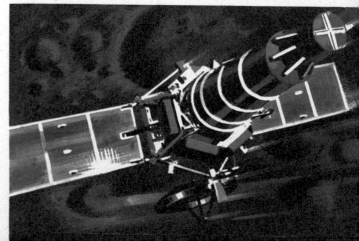

HISTORY IN SPACE

Some of the milestones of Man's explorations in Space.

Sputnik 1	4th October, 1957.	First orbiting space craft.
Sputnik 11	November, 1957.	Dog "Laika"; first living creature in orbit.
Luna 11	September, 1959.	Hard landing on the Moon.
Vostok 1	12th April, 1961.	First man in space—Yuri Gagarin.
Telstar	July, 1962.	First television satellite.
Vostok 6	June, 1963.	First woman in orbit
Voskhod 1	October, 1964.	Three men in orbit.
Voskhod 2	March, 1965.	First "space walk"
Early Bird	April, 1965.	First international communications satellite.
Mariner 4	July, 1965.	Close-up pictures of Mars.
Gemini 6-7	December, 1965.	First space rendezvous
Luna 9	February, 1966.	First (unmanned) soft landing on Moon.
Venus 3	March, 1966.	Hard landing on Venus.
Gemini 10	July, 1966.	First space docking.
Apollo 8	December, 1968.	First flight round the Moon.
Apollo 11	July, 1969.	First manned Moon landing.
Lunokhod	November, 1970.	First (unmanned) "Moon Rover".
Intelsat 4	January, 1971.	First major communications satellite
Soyuz 11/Salyut	June, 1971.	First "space station" in orbit.
Apollo 15	July, 1971.	Two-man "Moon Rover' used for exploration.
Pioneer 10	February, 1972.	First space craft intended to leave the solar system after flying past Jupiter.
Skylab	May, 1973.	Orbiting workshop launched.
Skylab 1.	May, 1973.	First Skylab crew is launched and carries on repairs aboard their craft.

The next step in manned space flight for both Russia and America was to launch two-man craft. The Russian Voskhod 2 flight on 18th March, 1965, included the first "space walk" when Alexei Leonov (above) left his craft by a special airlock tunnel and floated in space for ten minutes, 500 kilometres above the Earth. This was the first time that a man had trusted his life to a space suit and attempted to work in a weightless condition. Despite long months of hard, physical and mental training, Leonov was sweating profusely when he came in after ten mimutes in space.

On their planned route to the Moon, the Americans used their Gemini flights to answer a number of vital questions. A safe flight to the Moon, followed by a landing and return to Earth, depended on the ability of two space craft to meet accurately in orbit using radar and computers (and human flying skill). And it depended also on men doing their complex tasks efficiently after long periods in space. Both these major objectives were achieved by the Gemini flights.

And what, after all that history, is to come next?
Space craft from Earth are already blazing
trails out across the solar system, and early in
December, 1973, Pioneer 10 hurtled to within
81,000 miles of the giant planet Jupiter (see top
illustration). It sent back pictures and streams of
information to Earth which gave a terrifying taste
of the planet's intense and deadly radiation and
the nature of its turbulent cloudy structure.

Pioneer 10 has a very special place in history—it
will be the first man-made object to leave the
solar system. Crossing the orbit of Pluto (more
than 3.6 billion miles from the Sun) in 1987, it will
head on towards the region of the galaxy now
marked by the constellation, Taurus, which by the
time it arrives, millions of years in the future, will be

gone, its stars drifted apart or dead.

If it survives the cold immensity of space, it may
one day announce to another race of space
travellers that it came from Earth, for on its side it
carries a plaque engraved with drawings of a man
and a woman (and their size compared with
Pioneer 10), plus a diagram showing the solar
system's position in the galaxy.

Another trail-blazer is the Viking space craft
(above) due to land on Mars to celebrate the two
hundredth birthday of the United States on 4th
July, 1976. It will take pictures, scoop up soil
samples and analyse them in its own "mini-
laboratories." Its findings will be sent back to
Earth via a relay orbiter craft. Mainly, it will be searching for signs of life.

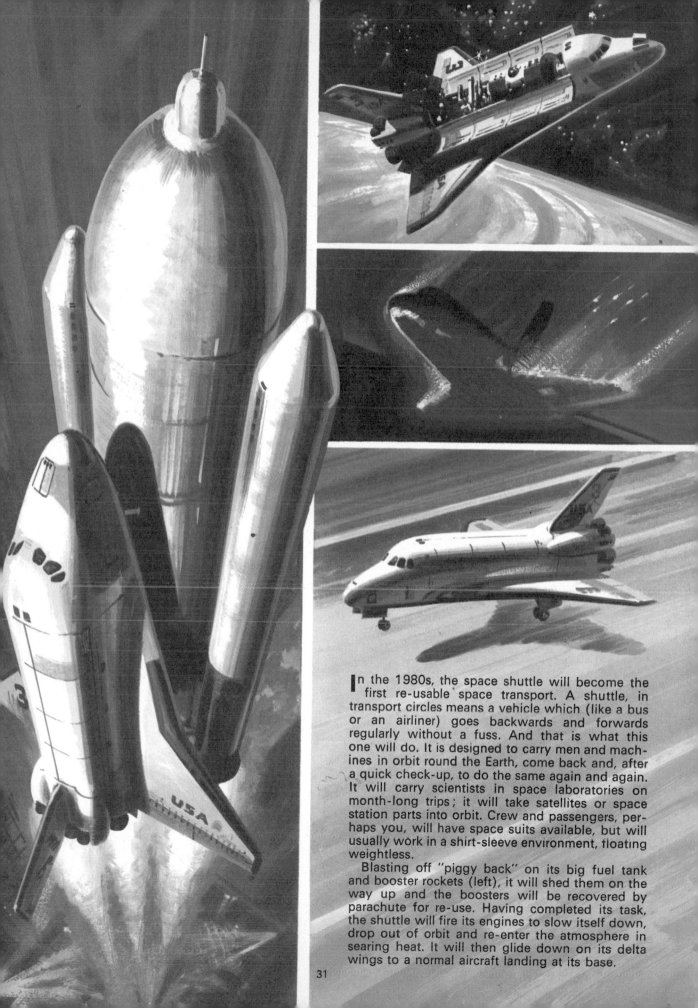

In the 1980s, the space shuttle will become the first re-usable space transport. A shuttle, in transport circles means a vehicle which (like a bus or an airliner) goes backwards and forwards regularly without a fuss. And that is what this one will do. It is designed to carry men and machines in orbit round the Earth, come back and, after a quick check-up, to do the same again and again. It will carry scientists in space laboratories on month-long trips; it will take satellites or space station parts into orbit. Crew and passengers, perhaps you, will have space suits available, but will usually work in a shirt-sleeve environment, floating weightless.

Blasting off "piggy back" on its big fuel tank and booster rockets (left), it will shed them on the way up and the boosters will be recovered by parachute for re-use. Having completed its task, the shuttle will fire its engines to slow itself down, drop out of orbit and re-enter the atmosphere in searing heat. It will then glide down on its delta wings to a normal aircraft landing at its base.

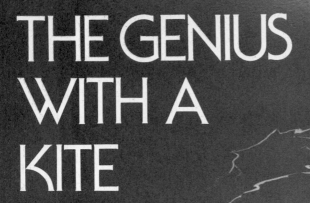

THE GENIUS WITH A KITE

What caused the brilliant flashes in the sky that people called lightning? Nobody knew until Benjamin Franklin decided to fly his kite in a storm.

Lightning zig-zagged through the black sky. Benjamin Franklin was eager and excited as he prepared to make a practical test of one of his scientific theories. To set off into the country in the middle of a fierce storm might seem a strange thing to do, but for the purpose which Franklin had in mind, conditions could not have been better.

He and his son went to a field outside Philadelphia, in the U.S.A., carrying a kite with a small pointed wire at the top to act as a lightning conductor. Ordinary string was attached to the kite, with a length of silk ribbon joined to the end to act as an insulator. At the point where the string and the silk joined, Benjamin attached a brass key.

The kite was sent up with Franklin firmly holding on to the ribbon. The silk had to be kept dry, so Franklin stood in a cowshed.

Brilliant flashes of lightning lit the scene for a brief second, for the storm was directly overhead. During one of the flashes, Franklin noticed that the fibres of the string were standing straight out, indicating that an electrical charge had collected on the string. With great care, he moved his hand towards the key. A spark of electricity jumped to his hand. Franklin had proved that lightning is caused by electrical discharges between clouds, or between clouds and the earth. We know that the air and the earth's surface are charged with electricity of opposite kinds—positive and negative—and that there is a constant interchange of electricity going on between them. Ordinarily this does not manifest itself as lightning because moist air is a fairly good conductor

When the air becomes dry, the interchange becomes more difficult with the result that the air becomes heavily charged and enormous quantities of electricity accumulate in the clouds. Finally, when the charge becomes so great that it can overcome the resistance of the atmosphere, the electricity leaps violently across the gap to hilltop, a church spire, house roof or to another cloud, and there is a great flash.

This is how lightning is produced. Until the time of this experiment—in 1752—no means existed of safeguarding houses from being burnt by fires caused by lightning striking them. Franklin suggested, however, that as lightning was simply caused by electricity seeking a path to earth, it would cause no damage if it were given a safe path to follow.

At his instigation, metal rods were fixed to the roofs of buildings and the tops of church spires. From each of these, a wire led down the side of the building and into the earth. Should a building be struck by lightning, the electricity would strike the rod and flow to earth harmlessly.

Nowadays, lightning conductors, as we now know them, are fixed to all

Sparks streamed from the key to Benjamin Franklin's hand. This experiment with a kite in a storm had confirmed his belief that lightning was electricity. In this picture, Franklin's work as a scientist is shown symbolically.

tall buildings, thanks to the experiments of Franklin and his kite.

Although he made a discovery of lasting value, Franklin was not wholly a scientist. It was not until 1746, when he was wealthy enough to be able to spare time from his business, that he could take up scientific research. Electricity at that time was a little understood phenomena, and Franklin was deeply interested in it. He had experimented with Leyden jars (ordinary glass jars covered inside and outside with silver paper) which were capable of storing a quantity of electricity until, on connecting the inner

and outer coatings, the charge was liberated in the form of a spark. It was this which led Franklin on to his work into the behaviour of lightning.

Benjamin Franklin's work was all the more surprising because he did not come from a scientific family. He was the tenth of seventeen children of a poor soap- and candle-maker. Born in Boston, U.S.A. in 1706, he spent his early youth helping in his father's business. Later, he was apprenticed to a printer.

In 1723, Franklin decided to go to Philadelphia to carve out a career for himself. He was hungry and penniless

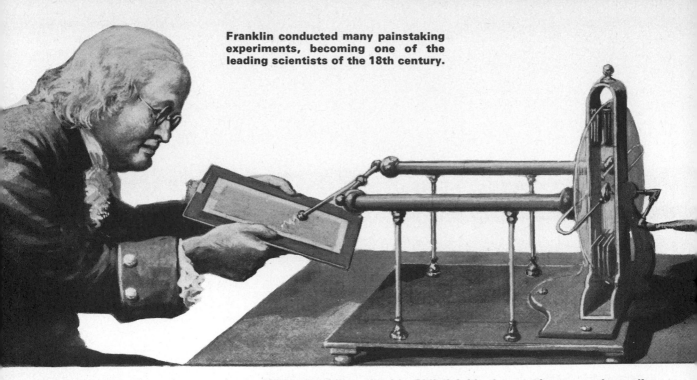

Franklin conducted many painstaking experiments, becoming one of the leading scientists of the 18th century.

when he arrived. But with great determination and perseverance he became the manager of a newspaper and travelled to England to gain experience in his profession. By the time he was thirty, he was clerk to the Pennsylvania Assembly. He progressed from postmaster of Philadelphia to deputy postmaster for all the American colonies. In twenty years, from his arrival, he rose to become the most important of Philadelphia's citizens.

Although he led a busy life as a diplomat and politician, he continued scientific experiments in various fields. When he was sent to England on a diplomatic mission in 1757, he was welcomed as a distinguished scientist as well as a diplomat, and was honoured by the universities of Oxford and St. Andrews, Scotland.

Among the things which Franklin worked upon were experiments concerned with the effects of lead upon the human constitution, the stilling of waves by pouring oil upon them, the varying extent to which clothes of different colours absorb heat and the characteristics of electricity.

Franklin suffered from gout in his later years, but he continued to play an important part in the affairs of his country. He was elected president of the commonwealth of Pennsylvania three times, and three times re-elected. He returned again to his scientific pursuits. His researches in electricity had won him a fellowship of the Royal Society of Britain as long ago as 1752.

In 1790, he died after a short illness at the age of eighty-four—a great American with an enquiring, scientific mind whose monument is the lightning conductor on every large building. Without it, lightning could be a destroyer instead of a brilliant and usually harmless flash in the sky.

When Franklin arrived in Philadelphia, he was hungry and penniless. But he was destined to become famous as a scientist and statesman.

In the field of scientific discovery and invention, some of the greatest victories have been won in the battle against disease and death. The story which began with simple remedies long ago continues today in the laboratory and operating theatre. Thanks to the advances which science has made during the present century, we have amassed a formidable armoury of weapons for this battle.

Disasters can be fought where they occur with mobile blood transfusion units, mobile operating theatres and even temporary hospitals which can be moved scores of miles and set up almost overnight for immediate use.

Today, doctors accomplish the miracle of repairing hearts—even transplanting them, with limited success—of giving new lenses to blind eyes and new beauty for lost features. They can excise a tumour buried deep in the vital tissues of the brain. They can isolate and control deadly infections which, a few decades ago, were still a cause for anxiety and a century ago, would have proved fatal.

Truly, we are living in a wonderful new age of medicine, and one of the most vital accomplishments of this lies in the field of what has been popularly called spare-parts surgery. Damaged joints can be replaced by nylon substitutes; new valves of plastic can be inserted in the heart; livers and other vital organs such as kidneys can be transplanted from donors, and artificial aids can also be used to help people to lead normal lives. Electronic pace makers inserted in the body stimulate the heart to maintain its regular beat. Machines can be installed in people's homes to enable them to carry out a normal life despite the malfunctioning of a liver. Artificial respirators keep paralysed people alive when their lung muscles are unable to make normal breathing possible.

Literally, thousands of people throughout the world might be dead or weak and bedridden were it not for the great advances in modern surgery made this century. But, inevitably, many of these successes have produced their human sadnesses.

The smiling face of this brave thalidomide boy driving his electric car is a symbol of the way in which science and medicine are bringing fuller lives to handicapped people.

HELPING THE HANDICAPPED

Accident victims, for example, restored to full health by the surgeon's skill, may be minus a limb. Deafness and blindness are, in many cases, incurable, and a person whose larynx has been removed has irretrievably lost the power of speech. But science is coming to the aid of these people.

False limbs have enabled the legless to walk again. Arms with electric "muscles" which move in a natural manner bring mobility to those so handicapped, and attempts have even been made to insert artificial voice boxes into the body to restore speech to those who have lost it. But

this is still in the experimental stage.

Striking experiments are being made in the restoration of sight to the blind. One of the most remarkable advancements in this direction was made in America where a midget television camera mounted on the frame of a pair of glasses, was worn by the blind person. The camera's signals were passed to a flexible corset worn around the waist. Woven into the corset was a six inch square matrix holding 256 electrodes.

These sent thousands of tingling electrical pulses to the skin, and the nervous system carried them to the brain. A blind person received these pulses as a crude, but recognisable, image of what was before him. In sighted

people, the eye's retina turns light rays into nerve signals which the brain converts into mental pictures. Like the retina, the skin contains a two-dimensional sheet of receivers which can transmit pattern information to the brain.

With this device, blind patients have been able to recognise people, identify objects and tell the difference between light and shadow. Dr. Carter Compton Collins, who is developing this, is also experimenting with similar sensing aids that would allow a deaf person to hear and an amputee to "feel" with an artificial limb.

Other aids for blind people are concerned with enabling them to hear sounds which tell them about obstacles in their path. For instance, there are sunglasses which send out a beam of infared rays. When these are reflected back by an object, a warning note is heard by the user. By moving his head from side to side or up and down, the blind person can tell where the object is and how big it is.

But there still exists the

Hope for people with weak hearts is offered by a nuclear powered pace maker, shown undergoing laboratory development on the left. At present, battery-powered pace-makers are replaced by surgery every two or three years, but this will operate for ten years.

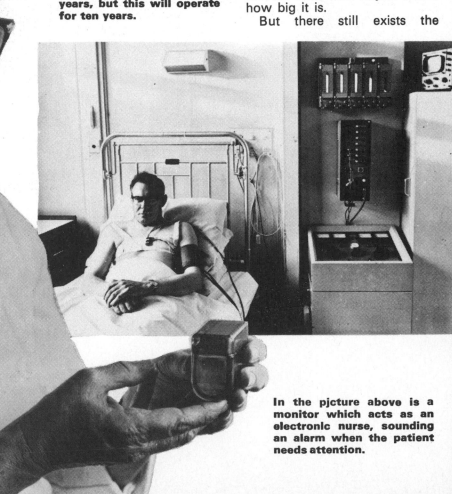

In the picture above is a monitor which acts as an electronic nurse, sounding an alarm when the patient needs attention.

36

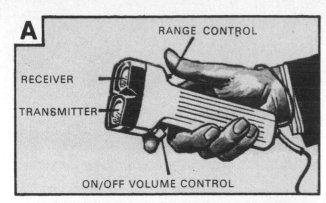

problem of enabling a blind person to read normal type. For this, there is a machine called the Optacon which is about the size of a shoulder-strap tape recorder. When the user runs a small photo-electric sensor (that looks like a tiny microphone) along a line of printed type, the letters are turned into shapes by tiny, vibrating pins which can be felt on the machine. By keeping his finger pressed tightly against the pins, the user can feel the shapes of the letters as the sensor is slid along the line of type.

Similar to this is the Optophone developed in Britain, which uses a moving beam of light to scan the printed words and turns them into sound tones, something like the Morse code.

Blind people can also move about freely with a sonic torch made by British scientists, most of them at the university of Birmingham. It sends out a beam of sound above our range of hearing (like a bat's high note) which is echoed back by objects in front of the walker. These are received in the torch and converted into sound which the user can hear through an earphone. With training, the user of a sonic torch can build up a mental picture of what lies ahead and detect people, trees, gateways and any other obstruction which

To help blind people, the sonic torch (A) has been developed. Instead of a beam of light, it makes a beam of sound too high for human ears to hear. These sound waves (B) are reflected by obstacles, received by the torch and converted into audible signals which are conveyed to the user through an earphone. A blind person using one (right) can build up a mental picture of the way ahead.

is too far away to be touched by his cane.

A disability that is as distressing as blindness is constant pain. People who suffer from this cannot work or sleep properly and are in perpetual agony from which drugs bring only temporary relief.

This has been tackled by a scientist, Dr. C. Norman Shealy of America, who based his approach on the knowledge that all sensations from the body are carried to the brain by the spinal cord. He inserted electrodes in a

patient's spinal cord and connected these with very fine wires to a receiver just below the skin of the abdomen. On the surface of the skin, a coil of wire was taped.

The coil was plugged into a battery-powered transmitter the patient carried in his shirt pocket. All that the patient had to do when he felt any pain was to switch on the transmitter. This caused electricity to flow into the coil of wire and induce a current in the receiver beneath the skin. The current flowed along the wires to the electrodes in the spinal cord.

As natural impulses in the spinal cord are electrical, it was thus possible to obliterate the pain-causing impulses and replace them with a buzzing or tingling sensation, like the feeling of a cat's throat when it purrs. Some patients get relief from pain in this way, but others find the sensation too annoying. In fact, some surgeons have had to remove the device because the patients objected to the feeling.

Fortunately, in many cases the pain-killer is successful and has reduced pain to about a quarter of what it was.

Such a breakthrough, though not perhaps sensational, is certainly an advancement towards the time when people with physical handicaps will be able to overcome them with the help of science. Perhaps the hardest to solve is the loss of speech caused by the removal of the larynx. One solution to this was a device that looked like a tobacco pipe. The stem was placed in the mouth and a button was pressed on the bowl. Sound waves came from the bowl and the dumb person learnt to control these waves with his breath.

As yet, we are only at the beginning of the solution to these and many other problems. But, certainly, the answers will be found. Research is continually going on and new theories are constantly being tested. We may well be amazed by even greater results in the years to come.

Disabled people can type (above left') by blowing through a tube connected to a special typewriter. A switch in the glasses (above), worked by the movement of the eyes, enables a paralysed person to control a wheelchair. Deaf children are learning to speak (below) with the help of a toy poodle which begs, stands up and walks when they speak into a microphone.

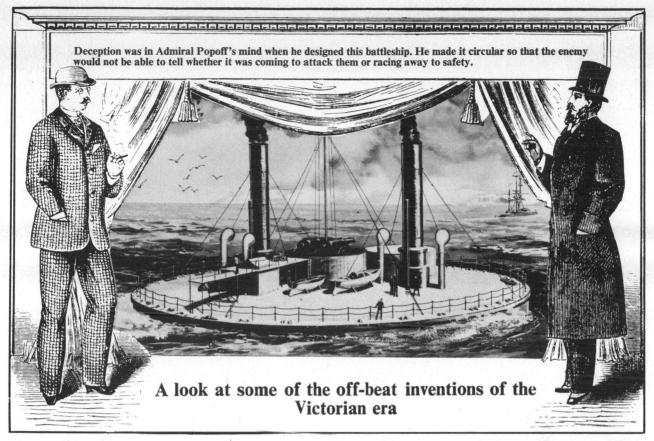

Deception was in Admiral Popoff's mind when he designed this battleship. He made it circular so that the enemy would not be able to tell whether it was coming to attack them or racing away to safety.

A look at some of the off-beat inventions of the Victorian era

Victorian Ventures

Invasion fleets approaching Britain would have been met by a line of forts like these, if William John Hall had had his way.

If strange hammering sounds come from the shed at the bottom of your neighbour's garden, do not be alarmed. Should occasional clouds of sulphur fumes waft your way or a dense fog of black smoke float across your house, try not to be perturbed. The man toiling away behind a locked door may be an amateur inventor. And the device he is perfecting may turn out to be as important a landmark in the history of mankind as the wheel, the internal combustion engine or the H-bomb. Or it may not!

Thousands of people in Britain every year apply for a patent for an invention. This is a form of legal protection to stop others copying their ideas. Of these thousands—there were 63,614 in 1969—only a small proportion may be good enough to be manufactured and sold. Some of them, indeed, may be so highly eccentric as to appeal to nobody else but their inventor. Of these, nothing will ever be known by the rest of us.

About a hundred years ago, however, in the Victorian era, inventors were just as wildly unorthodox as they presumably are today. And some of the things they invented seem to us strangely impractical. But then, we are seeing them with the eyes of a later age in which electronics and the various forms of power available nowadays make Victorian ideas, in contrast, appear fantastic.

But the Victorians had the courage of their con-

When this steam organ was played softly, it could be heard a hundred yards away. And when it was played loudly the hearers were lucky if their ear drums survived.

victions. Many of the strange things they created were advertised and offered for sale, or publicised in magazine articles. And their interests lay in war and transport, like those of today's inventors.

War at sea, for example, was a big subject. There was an Admiral Popoff in Russia who invented a round battleship, with the object of deceiving the enemy as to which way it was going. It was driven by six propellers and had guns which could fire in any direction. One of these ships made a long voyage in the Black Sea. Its sides rose only 18 inches out of the water and the deck, which was 100 ft. in diameter, curved upwards towards the middle, where it was five or six feet above the sea.

Not to be outdone, a British inventor countered with an underwater bomber. James Nasmyth designed a concrete vessel like a submarine with a bomb in its nose. This was meant to explode when its cap hit the side of a ship six feet under the water. But the helmsman, fireman and the two boilermen working the steam engine would have had a shattering time if it was ever used.

Any invader, foolhardy enough to brave such a device and approach our shores, would have been met by a hail of fire from an "impregnable iron fortress", if Mr. William John Hall had had his way. He proposed the use of a huge iron shell, shaped like an upturned cigar, set in concrete on the sea bed. Inside it, there would be 70 cannons firing through portholes at any enemy ship careless enough to come within range. On the top there was a light-house which was lowered into the shell when war-fare began.

A force of 1,500 men, recruited from the destitute wanderers in the streets of our cities, would have been required to fire the guns and bring up the ammunition from magazines formed in the solid concrete well below the water. Powder, shot and shells would be raised up a shaft, and everybody would be kept warm by steam rising through hollow columns supporting the floors.

Away from the horrors of war, other inventors were busy with their own fancies. Flying was one of these. There was a Belgian, Mr. de Groof, who jumped from the basket of a balloon over Epping Forest in Essex standing in a wooden framework to which wings were attached. It was a form of parachute which imitated a bat's wings and was guided by levers which were worked by hand. There were occasions when it worked—and one when it did not, and that was the end of both Mr. de Groof and his invention.

A safer idea was a floating bicycle which was like a canoe with outrider floats and pedals which turned a screw propeller. Even more down to earth was a metal seat which ladies could wear under their copious dresses and rest whenever the fancy took them.

Transport, however, was ever uppermost in the Victorians' minds. There was, for instance, a thing called an Impulsoria in which horses, galloping on a conveyor belt, drove the wheels, through gears, of a huge wagon on rails. Horse power was also in the mind of the man, William Francis Snowdon, who thought of a treadmill bus. Horses, tramping around and around on a turntable, made the bus move. How fast—and how far—is not recorded.

It must have been almost as frightening for the unsuspecting pedestrians to see as was an equally formidable device called an Aerophon. Fortunately,

Hooves cannot negotiate railway tracks, so this four horse-power locomotive was put forward as a means of hauling colliery trucks.

the Aerophon was stationary, because it was a steam organ and it was first heard in London in 1851 at the Great Exhibition. Steam was forced through pipes to make the music and, even when played softly, it could be heard for a hundred yards. After the exhibition, it was put in a ballroom where partners "danced by steam" every night.

But the crowning fantasy of the Victorian era—something we are certain was never made—was a bomb-shaped projectile as big as a bus. Fifteen people, sitting in this were to be dropped from the top of the Eiffel Tower in Paris into a specially-made pond below.

The inventor spoke about the occupants as having an "emotional descent". That was a master-piece of understatement.

Not all inventions during the Victorian era, which lasted for more than 63 years from 1837, were as out-of-the-ordinary as the ones described here.

Among the important things which happened was the introduction of the penny post, the first satisfactory submarine telegraph cable was laid between Dover in England and Calais in France, a big steamship, the "Great Eastern" was launched, antiseptic surgery was introduced by Joseph Lister, the first successful incandescent electric light was produced by Thomas Edison in America and Joseph Swan in Britain, and in France Louis Pasteur was making experiments in immunisation against disease.

Other things that happened during Queen Victoria's reign were the production of the first motor car, the discovery of X-rays and the achievement by Marconi of the transmission of a message by wireless for over a mile. Meanwhile, in America, Alexander Graham Bell was making experiments which led to the first telephone.

Clearly, we owe much to the great inventors of the Victorian era. The results of their work are with us today, but we must be thankful that the crazier ideas of the more off-beat inventors died merciful deaths in their infancy.

A Belgian inventor jumped from a balloon wearing these wings. At first they worked, but there was a final, fatal occasion when they did not.

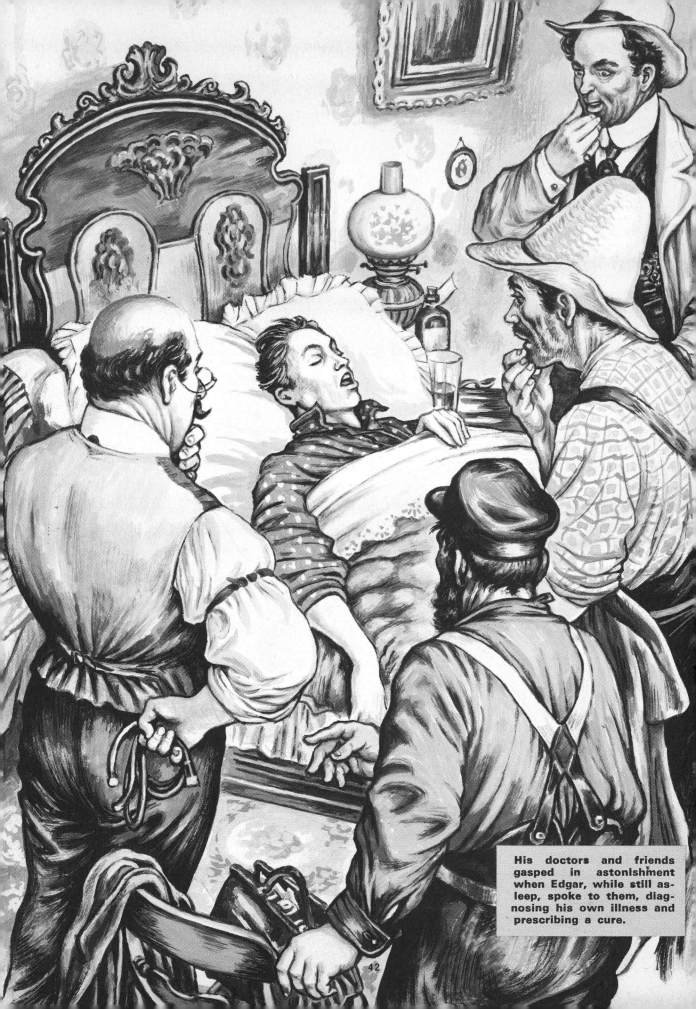

His doctors and friends gasped in astonishment when Edgar, while still asleep, spoke to them, diagnosing his own illness and prescribing a cure.

He Cured People In His Sleep

The young man lay down on the sofa. He removed his tie, loosened his collar, untied his shoes, and laid his hands on his stomach. Slowly he closed his eyes. His breathing gradually deepened until, after a final deep breath, he was apparently fast asleep.

A second man, who had been sitting in the far corner of the room, arose and approached the sleeping man saying: "Imagine that before you isthe body of the child Aime Dietrich who resides in this house. You will go over this child's body carefully. Examine it thoroughly and tell me the disability you find at the present time. Give the cause of this disability, also suggestions for the help and relief of this child. You will speak distinctly, at a normal rate of speech. You will answer the questions I will ask."

For the past three years, little Aime had been thought incurable. At the age of two, she had contracted influenza but, after having apparently recovered, she became the victim of violent convulsions. Over the years, they had grown steadily worse until by the time she was five she was having as many as twenty fits a day. Without warning she would suddenly fall over, and her whole body would stiffen until it was completely rigid. Numerous doctors and specialists had been called in, but to no avail.

Mrs. Dietrich had given up all hope of her daughters' recovery. And then someone told her about Edgar Cayce, who lived in the nearby state of Kentucky. This man had been accredited with some miraculous cures which he administered while in a hypnotic trance. Maybe he could cure Aime. Could this uneducated man succeed where the best medical brains in the country had failed?

"Yes, we have the body." The sleeping Edgar Cayce spoke in a deep, authoritative voice completely alien to his normal shy mannerisms. He announced that the day before Aime had caught influenza she had had a fall which had injured her spine. It was this injury that was responsible for the attacks. He gave instructions for relieving the pressure at the base of the spine.

Mrs. Dietrich agreed that the girl had fallen as Edgar had stated, but only she and Aime knew of it. The fall had been so minor, and Aime did not appear to be hurt, so neither of them had thought any more about it.

An osteopath was called to to perform the operation ordered by Edgar Cayce, and the following day another hypnotic session was conducted. Edgar announced that the surgical adjustment had not been made correctly and so another operation was performed, but it was still not to the sleeping man's satisfaction. A third operation was undertaken and the following morning Edgar announced that it had been successful.

Within a week, Aime's mind began to funtion normally again. Soon she had regained the menttal ability of a normal five year old. Aime Dietrich and her family were able to lead a normal life once again. The trouble never reappeared.

Edgar Cayce's curative powers first came to light when he was twenty-three years old. One day in March, 1900, he went to his local doctor for a sedative as he was suffering from a severe headache. He took the medicine and lost consciousness. The next thing he knew he was back home in bed. A friend had found him wandering the streets in a daze. The doctor's medicine had been too strong and Edgar's

voice had faded to a faint and painful whisper. He fell into a deep coma, his body being tormented by a high fever. Doctors tried in vain to bring him back to consciousness, but there was nothing that they could do!

The doctors had given up all hope when suddenly Edgar, although still asleep, started to speak in a voice that was loud and clear. They could hardly believe their ears when the young man told them what was wrong with him. He instructed them to prepare a paste of certain ingredients, which they were to rub on his back at the base of the spine. Filled with incredulity, but prepared to try anything to restore their patient's health, the doctors followed the instructions. Within a short time, Edgar was back to health and none the worse for his unusual experience.

Many people urged him to produce some more miraculous cures, but he was opposed to the idea until a friend became ill Edgar went into a trance and, speaking in Latin (a language which he had never seen or heard of before that day), gave the medical men a precise prescription. Treated with the medicine made up from the prescription, his friend was declared cured a week later. From that day on, Edgar was persuaded to allow himself to be hypnotised twice a day in order to diagnose the ailments of the many apparently incurable people that now flocked to see him. His diagnoses and prescriptions were invariably correct and he often recommended cures that were unknown to the medical profession.

On one occasion he prescribed "Oil of Smoke" for a patient. The local doctors and chemists had never heard of it. It was not listed in any pharmaceutical catalogues. Edgar was hypnotised again and gave the name of a chemists shop in a town several miles distant.

A telegram was sent to the store owner, but he had not heard of the medication either A third hypnotic session was arranged and this time the retailer was told to look on a particular shelf behind a certain container. There, sure enough, he found the required bottle. Its label was stained and faded. The company that made the substance had long since ceased operations, and the store owner had no idea that it was there !

Edgar Cayce was born in Hopkinsville, a small farming community in Kentucky, U.S.A. on 18 March, 1877. As a child he showed no signs of the power that lay locked within his brain In fact, he did rather badly at school and never really completed his education. And yet, he was to become one of the most sought after medical practioners in America. He had absolutely no knowledge of medicine or biology but under hypnosis he was able to prescribe successful cures for ailments that orthodox doctors had been unable to treat. He did not have to see the patient; a photograph, some personal memento, or just a letter was sufficient to release his mysterious powers.

For forty-three years, Edgar Cayce practised medical diagnosis in this way. By the time of his death on 5 January, 1945, over 30,000 written case histories testified to his achievements. No other psychic medium has left such well documented proof of his or her power. It is not known how this uneducated man was able to prescribe accurately for illnesses that had perplexed the best doctors in America. And to this day scientists remain baffled by the strange case of Edgar Cayce—the man who cured people in his sleep.

What was the mysterious ailment which afflicted little Aime Dietrich? Only Edgar Cayce, lying in a hypnotic trance, was able to identify it and describe the correct treatment.

44

Feeding the Hungry Millions

To save millions from starvation, scientists are finding ways of manufacturing food from unfamiliar ingredients.

Relief for starving children, like that being provided here by United Nations workers in Africa, brings only a temporary respite from the universal food shortage.

Look at a map of the world and put your finger on any of the following places: India, Bangladesh, Java, Egypt, the Middle East, the Western Sahara, the Caribbean and Brazil, and then trace the Andes from Chile to Mexico.

Now sit back and take a deep breath, for yours has been a finger of death; in all those places, people are dying not spasmodically from riots, wars, feuds or murder but consistently from starvation. For in these—and the under-developed countries as a whole—between three and five hundred million people are undernourished or suffering from hunger. And about 1,600 million people are regularly undernourished, which means that they are starved of protein. This is a complicated organic chemical which is found in foods like meat, fish, eggs and cheese. In some countries, such as India, there are millions of men, women and children who hardly ever eat food containing protein at all.

To stay healthy, human beings must eat at least a small amount of protein every day of their lives.

45

Unfortunately, man and nature are sadly out of harmony as far as the production of protein-containing food is concerned. The proteins that we need are supplied by chickens that lay eggs, cows that give milk and fish that are caught in the sea.

But chicks are not hatched from eggs, calves are not born and fish do not spawn every day in every part of the world where proteins are so desperately needed.

The argument for scientists who are concerned about the world shortage is a simple one. "Why is it not possible to manufacture proteins in factories which could be built anywhere in the world?"

In the future, scientists may be able to prove that this is possible. For a long time, they have been looking for new and better ways of making proteins from materials which are cheap and easily available.

In Canada, the bones, skin and heads of fish are dried and purified to make protein powder, which is odourless and tasteless. In Japan, protein is being made from seaweed, while in Britain a new protein powder is being made from potatoes, sugar, fat and other cheap foods which normally contain little or no protein.

Mixed with flavouring substances, these can become an acceptable food to people in the under developed countries which need it so badly.

People in the West Indies found it difficult to know what to do with a strange material called bagasse. This is a tough, wooden fibre left behind when sugar is extracted from sugar cane. Some of

Protein is an important constituent of food. It can be obtained from seaweed (seen being blanched in the top picture) and from fish, some of which are being specially bred in ponds like the one shown above in Java.

it was burnt in the ovens used to boil the sugar-sap from the cane, but most of it was simply thrown away.

Now a method of making proteins from the millions tons of of bagasse which are produced every year has been discovered. Bagasse contains an important chemical called cellulose, which is also found in wood, grass and straw. Cellulose is a kind of natural plastic (in fact, a compound of cellulose was formerly used to make photographic film).

Human stomachs simply cannot digest cellulose, which is the main reason why we cannot eat grass as cows do. But the fact that cows' stomachs can digest cellulose in grass and hay has given scientists the clues they need as to how to make proteins from the cellulose in bagasse and, indeed, from wood, straw and other substances which contain cellulose.

The bagasse is ground to a pulp in water, using grinding machines. The pulp is then placed in huge, stainless steel vats and special strains or breeds of bacteria are added.

The bacteria multiply and grow in their millions in the watery pulp, giving off chemicals which can digest the cellulose in the bagasse and change it into protein.

Bagasse protein is a grey powder which is completely without smell or taste and yet it is highly nutritious. Pound for pound, this powder can supply humans with more protein than steak or cheese.

Scientists have been able to make very tasty hamburgers and sausages from bagasse by mixing the powder with colouring and flavouring with water and cereals to give the mixture some substance, known as texturing.

Colouring, flavouring and texturing protein is now a branch of science in its own right. The idea is to make the resultant food acceptable to the people for whom it is intended. In this way, they will be able to have nourishing food made with flavours with which they are familiar.

Protein can be made in oil refineries. One of the materials made in these is paraffin, of which certain grades contain a wax which must be removed before the paraffin can be used as a fuel for jet engines.

By using yeast, which is also used in the making of bread, this wax can be digested to form proteins. Yeast, like bacteria, multiplies and grows, giving off digestive chemicals. So now, food can be made in oil refineries by simply adding extra equipment for the digestion of wax.

Research work in this connection is advanced and it should only be a matter of time before oil refineries throughout the world are making a contribution to the food needs of the hungry millions.

There will, of course, be problems of distribution and payment—for the hungry are penniless as well as virtually foodless—but in this respect there will be a chance for the wealthy nations to support the poorer ones.

The need is urgent. How many people will die of starvation before a way is found of overcoming the world shortage of food?

Above: a scientist examines growing rice in a bid to improve the yeilds.
Right: a method of maknig protein in an oil refinery.

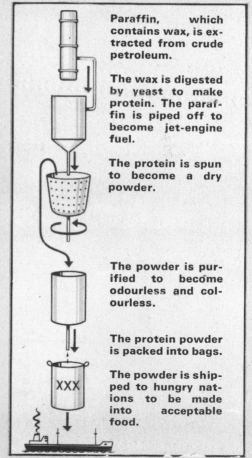

Paraffin, which contains wax, is extracted from crude petroleum.

The wax is digested by yeast to make protein. The paraffin is piped off to become jet-engine fuel.

The protein is spun to become a dry powder.

The powder is purified to become odourless and colourless.

The protein powder is packed into bags.

The powder is shipped to hungry nations to be made into acceptable food.

SCIENCE QUIZ

Now that you have read the science section of this book, see how many of the questions you can answer in the quiz below. The answers are at the back of the book.

1. A space craft is destined to leave the solar system and approach another galaxy, arriving millions of years in the future. What is the name of this space craft?

2. On which planet is the Viking space craft due to land in celebration of the two hundredth birthday of the United States on 4th July, 1976.

3. What were (a) the world's first artificial satellite, (b) the first living creature to go into space and (c) the first American satellite to go into orbit?

4. What was the name of the Russian space craft which took the first pictures of the far side of the Moon?

5. Who was (a) the first man in space and (b) the first woman in space? From which country were their flights launched?

6. What is the name of the device which is inserted into a person's body to stimulate the heart to maintain its regular beat?

7. Equipment incorporating a TV camera can enable a blind person to see in a limited way. How are the signals from this carried by the body to the brain?

8. Another aid for the blind is the Optacon. What does this enable the user to do?

9. A machine is being developed to deaden certain impulses carried by the spinal cord to the brain. What is the purpose of this machine?

10. To stay healthy, human beings must eat at least a small amount of a certain substance every day. What is this substance?

11. Food can be made in an industrial process by adding extra equipment for the digestion of wax. What substance has to be added and what is the nature of the industrial process?

12. Who was the man who took a kite out in a thunderstorm and discovered the nature of electricity? What invention resulted from this?

13. When little Aime Dietrich lay ill, who diagnosed her illness while he was in a trance-like sleep? Did he diagnose his own illness in this way?

14. Who invented a round battleship with the object of deceiving the enemy as to which way it was going?

15. An underwater bomber was devised by a British inventor. What was his name and what was his invention meant to do?

16. A Belgian jumped from a balloon in a framework to which wings were attached. What happened to the inventor on his last jump?

17. An emotional descent was promised to the passengers in a projectile dropped from a high tower in France. What was the name of the tower?

18. What was the name of the first television relay satellite and when did it transmit its first pictures?

19. Do you know the name of the device which sends out a beam of sound at a high pitch and enables blind people to move about freely in the streets?

20. In the West Indies a material, once wasted, is now used for making food. Can you say what this is?

As the war in Europe drew to a close, the focus of attention turned towards the conflict in the East. It was 1945 and the world was about to witness the drama of . . . .

THE BATTLE FOR THE PACIFIC

Death held no fears for Japanese pilots in the Pacific front during the Second World War. With only seconds to live, they would dive their bomb-laden planes at American aircraft carriers and other warships.

Such men were called "kamikaze". The Americans knew them as suicide pilots for they were, in effect, living bombs who aimed their plane at its target and died in the explosion that followed.

This method of attack was very successful both in the damage it caused and for its effect upon the morale of the American sailors and soldiers.

Three American aircraft carriers were heavily damaged by the diving "kamikazes" when they made a raid on Japan in 1945. Once the Americans had become established on Okinawa, they were subject to the suicide attacks.

Japanese suicide pilots failed to sink the U.S. aircraft carrier "Franklin", but explosions of octane spirit and ammunition killed over 800 of the crew.

General Douglas MacArthur, commander of America's army forces in the Pacific area (left). Emperor Hirohito of Japan (right) who visited MacArthur after the surrender.

Half of the 700 Japanese aircraft employed during the campaign were "kamikazes" and though most were destroyed before they could reach their targets, the remainder sank thirteen American destroyers.

Nor was the "kamikaze" principle confined to the air. On 6th April, the Japanese battleship "Yamato" set sail for her date with destiny.

The "Yamato" was sent to Okinawa to seek battle with the American fleet. With her, steamed a small destroyer escort, but no air cover was provided for the mighty vessel.

And the "Yamato" only carried

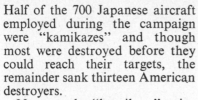

In their advance on Japan, the Americans stormed and captured many small islands (above). All the time, Douglas "Dauntless" planes (right) provided air cover. These effectively sank Japan's last modern battleship, "Yamato" in 1945 as it led a suicide force in support of an enemy counter-attack on Okinawa. The "Yamato" was believed to have been absolutely superior in guns, speed and armour to any other ship, but without air cover these great assets were of no avail. The pointless loss of this ship in a special attack on the Okinawa landings emphasises the straits to which the Japanese navy had been reduced at this stage of the war.

sufficient fuel for the outward voyage. No arrangements had been made for her return.

The following day, American carrier aircraft located the giant ship and pounded her to scrap with bombs and torpedoes and with a tremendous loss of life among her crew.

Okinawa fell after three months fighting with the loss of 110,000 Japanese compared with 49,000 Americans, the Japanese commander and his staff committing suicide rather than surrender.

In fact, Japan was already beaten. The end was only a matter of time. American submarines had sunk nearly five million tons of her shipping, which was a disaster for a country that depended so heavily upon imports of war materials.

Tokyo was almost obliterated on the night of 9th March when a "fire storm" swept away a quarter of a million buildings, killing and maiming 185,000 civilians.

The Okinawa landing brought about the overthrow of Japan's "pro-war" government and its replacement by one in favour of peace. But the main obstacle to a quick peace was the Allies' insistence on unconditional surrender. And as the months dragged on it looked as if the Japanese homeland would have to be invaded after all.

But no allied soldiers died on the beaches of Yokohama. On 6th August, a single B.29 bomber flew over Hiroshima and dropped an atomic bomb that wiped out a quarter of its inhabitants. Three days later, an even larger bomb was dropped on Nagasaki.

The Second World War officially ended when the Japanese instrument of surrender was signed with considerable pomp and ceremony aboard the U.S.S. "Missouri" in Tokyo Bay. This was on 2nd September, 1945, six years and one day after the war had begun with Germany's attack on Poland.

Hopping from island to island the Allies reached Okinawa in June, 1945.

(Red indicates Japanese expansion to January, 1943.)

The Magic of the Olympics

Finally, the five Olympic rings, representing the five continents, denote universal brotherhood, the Olympic ideal which is — and should be — basic to all human endeavour.

Once every four years, an ancient ceremony is re-enacted in the ruins of the temple of Zeus at Olympia, in Greece. A concave mirror is used to direct the sun's rays to light a torch held by a young maiden. Another young girl carries the flame to a bowl of gleaming white marble standing beside the river Alpheus. Then the first of a relay of athletes kindles a torch, linking the ancient and modern Olympic Games, that is to be carried to the country where the Games are being held.

The first Games of which we have record were held in 776 BC, although there is evidence that even then they had been in existence for over a hundred years. All wars in Greece ceased during the period of the Games and athletes from all over the country travelled to Olympia to compete. Like the modern Games, there were no expensive prizes for the winners, the ultimate victor received only a wreath of wild olive. But to the man that won it, it was a prize of infinite value.

The three main events of the ancient Games were races run over distances of one, two, and 25 stades. A stade was a straight track, 192.27 metres long, at each end of which were posts around which the athletes ran.

During the fourth century AD, invaders destroyed the city of Olympia and the Games ceased. Earthquakes buried the city under a sea of mud and it was not seen again until archeologists excavated the area in the 19th century. It was this discovery and excavation that kindled the spark to revive the Olympics. The modern Games, brought into

The modern Olympic Games (symbolised on the left) are a revival of the ancient games which are said to have their origin in a mythical chariot race between two early athletes (right).

The podium, at the top, indicates the crowning glory for the winners as well as their spirit of chivalry on the way to victory. Symbolic of man's perfection, it also represents the graphic interpretation of the letter M, the first letter of Montreal.

An easy "winner" of the 1904 marathon was Fred Lorz who was disqualified after hitching a lift.

being through the determined effort of Baron Pierre de Coubertin of France, date from 1896. They were held in Athens near the site of the original Games and, since 1896, have been held every four years with the exception of 1916, 1940, and 1944 when two World Wars intervened. The opening and closing ceremonies, features of the ancient Olympics, provide suitably stirring spectacles at the start and finish of the modern Olympics.

One event that is always full of surprises is the marathon. This did not form part of the old Games but was conceived in 1896 in memory of Pheidippides, who ran twenty-six miles from Marathon to Athens, having already run the distance twice that day, to carry the news of an Athenian victory.

Appropriately, the first winner of the modern marathon was a Greek, Spiridion Loues, a shepherd from the hills that overlook the Olympic arena. As he entered the stadium the crowd, who had witnessed no Greek wins during the preceding events, went wild with excitement. Two members of the Greek royal family, unable to contain their mounting jubilation, ran alongside their new-found hero all the way to the finishing line. The win was a surprise to the Greeks and the marathon has been a source of continual surprise ever since. Several runners have collapsed on the finishing straight; many have taken the wrong turning when entering the arena; and one man even hitched a lift on a car to be the first runner into the stadium! Needless to say, he was disqualified.

There is no doubt that the 1976 marathon in Montreal will have some shocks in store. Sport has always been popular in Montreal, both at the amateur and professional levels, and over the years the city has equipped itself with the facilities and resources that reflect its young and dynamic population. In fact, long before the Games of the twenty-first Olympiad had been awarded to Montreal by the International Olympic Committee, even before Pierre de Coubertin had rekindled the Olympic flame in 1896, Montreal had already demonstrated the spirit that is so much a part of the Olympic Games.

Montreal presented its own version of the Olympics in the 1840s, some fifty years before the first Games of modern times. Though modest in size, they were carefully planned and supervised and included many events which, in 1976, will attract the greatest athletes of the world, such as the high jump, the long jump, the triple jump, the hammer and discus throws, sprints of 100 and 400 yards, a mile race, and many other contests originally held at the first Olympic Games.

Young people from all over the world will be attending the 1976 Olympics, gathering at the youth camp that will be held for three weeks. It is expected that over a thousand people aged from 16 to 21 will participate in its programme of sports and cultural events. Youth camps have been a feature of the modern Olympics since 1921. At first they mainly attracted Boy Scouts, but today their purpose is to enable young people from around the globe to fraternise during the Games, attend the Games, and get to know the host city and surrounding country, thus encouraging development of the Olympic spirit in

At the heart of the emblem, the simplicity and the dignity of the Olympic stadium's track imply man's faith in an ideal.

Berlin was host to the Olympic Games in 1936, but Adolf Hitler, Germany's dictator, (right), clearly showed his disapproval when black athletes gained successes against Germany's white "mastermen".

The emblem for the Games of the XX1 Olympiad illustrates the human element stressed by Baron Pierre de Coubertin, founder of the modern Olympics.

the younger generation.

The Montreal Olympics will be housed in one of the most remarkable sports arenas in the world, designed by Frenchman Robert Taillibert. It will include two Olympic swimming pools, a special diving pool, a velodrome for cycling events, and a stadium which is designed so that it can be covered in winter. This will be used after the Games to stage American-style football and for the Montreal Expos baseball team. Seats can be adjusted for different sports by being glided round the stadium on an air cushion. The stadium, the main building of the Olympic complex, will accommodate 70,000 spectators during the Games.

The organisers have left nothing to chance. They have even consulted the weather men to ensure that everything is as perfect as it can be during the Games. They have reached the conclusion that the sun should be shining every day due to a long tradition that when Montreal has a celebration good weather always joins the party. And that should be a good omen for the success of the Games.

Many Olympic stars became stars in other fields like Johnny Weismuller, a swimmer who became a film Tarzan, and boxer Muhammad Ali, who became a world famous personality as well as heavyweight champion of the world.

56

England's First King

Mysteries abound in Britain's history, and one of the most intriguing of these concerns the man who was the first king of England and gave the country its name.

We know who he was, where he ruled before he set out on the conquests that were to make him the master of England, and where he learnt the arts of war. But we know little of the man himself (depicted on page 57), the man who with Saxon blood coursing through his veins was one of the mightiest warriors of all time.

His name was Egbert, sometimes written Ecgbert or Ecgberht, and he was an Anglo-Saxon, a member of one of the tribes which came from northern Germany and Jutland after the Romans left. The Saxons founded the kingdoms of Wessex, Sussex, Essex, Middlesex and Mercia. The Angles founded the eastern kingdoms of Northumbria and East Anglia.

The Anglo-Saxons lived in farms protected by a stockade and a moat, eating and sleeping in the hall. And the young men learnt how to shoot with bows and arrows and how to hunt with hawks. When they became men, they fought with shields and spears in the defence of their homes.

Mercia, in which Egbert lived, was a kingdom in the Midlands. From an early age, Egbert must have shown himself as a courageous fighter and a leader; but he was obviously regarded as a trouble maker—a potential rival— by the king of Mercia. He was disliked, too, by the king of Wessex, which lay in parts of the West Country. Perhaps they could see in Egbert a leader who would try one day to snatch their power. Whatever the reason, these two kings drove Egbert from Britain.

Egbert went to France, where he joined Charlemagne,

king of the Franks, who was ruling much of western Europe. Originally, Charlemagne's kingdom had been situated where Germany is today on the banks of the Rhine. But in 40 years he had spread his kingdom by successful wars to create a Christian Europe. His empire comprised Gaul, Italy and large parts of Spain and Germany.

Such a man must have fired Egbert with the zeal to return to his own country and take vengeance upon those who had banished him. Perhaps, when he was fighting with Charlemagne's armies against the Lombards or other tribes, he dreamed of conquering Britain and creating his own empire on this island.

For 13 years, Egbert fought with Charlemagne, perhaps all the time mentally planning campaigns against the original Britons—the Welsh—with the intention of creating an Anglo-Saxon Britain in his homeland.

His opportunity came in 802 when Beorhtric, the king of Wessex, died. Egbert returned to Britain in that year and took the vacant throne. Whether he took it by force, intrigue or by rightful descent is one of the mysteries with which early British history abounds.

However, once settled in his kingdom he set about moulding the Anglo-Saxon men into a tough army, able to fight with arrows and spears and to display courage and ruthlessness in battle. All the things he had learnt from Charlemagne were

put to good use.

Egbert had a two-fold ambition. One was to become the overlord of all the British kingdoms, and the other was to drive the Welsh out of the country.

Years of incessant wars followed. Egbert conquered Kent, Surrey, Sussex and Essex. He drove the Welsh out of Cornwall and captured their kingdom. Ten years later, he fought the Welsh again, this time at Camelford where he defeated them with the help of an army from Devon, as shown in the picture on this page.

Hardly was this battle over, when Egbert had to fight a terrific battle near Winchester against the Mercians where, so the historians tell us, "the slaughter was great on both sides" and "blood ran in rivers."

By 829, Egbert had become the first king to hold almost the whole of what is now England. He had seven Saxon kingdoms under his control, and decided that this large territory should bear the name of Engla land (the land of the Angles), which has since become England.

However, Egbert was not the immediate ruler of all these kingdoms, for each had its own king. The first man to be the true king of England was Egbert's grandson, Alfred the Great, who ruled over nearly the whole of England, except some parts that were held by the Danes.

Great power was held at this time by the Church. Charlemagne in Europe had made the Church his ally and had spread Christianity. Egbert took another leaf out of Charlemagne's book and did the same. Canterbury was the headquarters of the Church in England, and it was here that Egbert met the bishops and made a treaty of perpetual alliance with them.

But there were still the Welsh to be considered. Most of them had been driven into what is now Wales or across the channel to Brittany. Egbert was fed up with their raids into his territory and he made an ultimatum to them.

They would have to stay behind Offa's Dyke, an earth wall with a moat that ran from north to south from the mouth of the Dee to the Severn near Chepstow. Sentence of death would be passed automatically on any Welshman who crossed the dyke. And all people of Welsh blood had to leave his territory—or be killed.

Nevertheless, peace did not come readily to England. Egbert had to repel invasions from the Danes, and sometimes the Welsh and the Danes united in an effort to drive out the Saxons.

Egbert died in 839 and England's first king passed into history.

William's sisters had to help with the housework, although most of the work at the farm was done by servants.

A DAY IN STUART ENGLAND

At sunset on a winter's day in 1670, a boy was riding home from school on a little pony. His name was William Smith, he was ten years old and he was glad to be out of the grammar school. But he was also glad that he would return there the next morning.

There were no girls in William's school. In fact, his sisters could barely read or write. If a girl could cook and wash clothes, it seemed a waste of time to teach her more.

William's father was a yeoman, like many of his neighbours. He owned his land and was quite independent. Other farmers paid rent to big landowners.

William's home stood at the edge of the village, not far from the church, the inn and the smithy. All the other houses in the village were little cottages, down-at-heel and neglected. The men who lived in them were labourers who worked on nearby farms and always seemed to be very poor.

John Smith, William's father, did not rank as a gentleman, but he was entirely his own master. He voted at each election to Parliament, and since he voted openly, not by secret ballot, several other yeomen always voted as he did.

Whenever lots were drawn to find a recruit for the militia, he was among the chosen. That was a tribute to his position. However, John Smith always hired a penniless labourer to do his military service for him, and everyone was satisfied. The militia got a contented recruit, the recruit got extra pay and John Smith escaped service. The lots were always fixed beforehand to produce this result.

William Smith's farmhouse home was a neat square of brick with a tiled roof and large glazed windows. Except that it had no bathrooms or lavatories, it might have been a house of the present day.

The walls were panelled inside with wood, pleasantly carved, and the furniture was so well made that we would prize it today.

William joined the family for supper in the dining room. He had had a good midday meal at the grammar school, but he was looking forward to his supper of boiled chicken with sausages and bacon. Each portion was served on an individual pewter or earthenware plate, and everyone ate with his own personal knife and fork.

Clearly, life under the Stuarts was good for the young and strong in well-to-do families when England's future seemed good.

Britain had just about all the problems it could handle. There had been the great plague in 1665, which had killed thousands of people, and the great fire in 1666 when most of London had been turned into ashes. And to cap it all, there was trouble with the Dutch whose navy was harassing British ships in the English Channel.

Trade rivalry between the two nations was behind the problem, and it sparked off a four-day battle between the two navies from 1st to 4th June, 1666.

It occurred during a series of wars Britain was having against the Dutch. The first had broken out in 1652 followed by the second in 1664. As part of their manoevres during the second Dutch war, the British navy was in the English Channel with 80 ships under two admirals, the Duke of Albemarle and Prince Rupert.

Hearing that the French had declared war and were sending a squadron to attack them, the British dispatched a squadron to meet the French.

While this was absent, the Dutch attacked the British and for four days the two navies were attempting to destroy each other in a deadly battle. The British method was to form a line of ships like a cavalry line and to keep to this formation rigidly while it attacked the enemy.

The Dutch, on the other hand, advanced like cavalry, but allowed their ships to leave their ranks and to charge their enemy separately.

This battle was a landmark in British naval history, for it taught them that their formal line of battle was the best, and it was to gain them many successes in the years that were to follow.

Things were going badly for the British, when the squadron which had been sent to meet the French returned without having encountered them.

But despite these reinforcements, the Dutch were winning and the British finally retired into the Thames after losing twenty ships.

However, in later battles, the Dutch were defeated and the two countries made a peace pact in 1667. A further war from 1672 to 1674 ended with a treaty of friendship between the British and the Dutch.

As if the plague and the great fire of London were not trouble enough, Britain had to marshall a fleet to tackle a Dutch invasion.

THE MENACE
IN THE CHANNEL

PASTIMES OF THE PAST

Football (left) is an ancient game. An inflated pig's bladder was undoubtedly an early football. As long ago as the middle ages, the bladder was covered with leather and primitive rules were observed.

The idea of hitting a ball with a stick arrived in early times (above). Many of our modern games such as hockey, hurling and shinty probably developed from them. Bowls (right) is one of the oldest of British sports and was known in 1299.

Studious, bespectacled youths poring thoughtfully over chess boards; jolly mums having a fling at bingo; slim, healthy youngsters in white leaping with their rackets in a spirited game of tennis . . . they are all up-to-the-minute people passing the time in the way which gives them most pleasure. But there is nothing up-to-the-minute about the things they are doing for these pastimes. like most of the others we take part in, are as old as the hills

Once, for example, King Charles VIII of France saw stars—and no wonder. He had just hit his head aginst the lintel of his palace as he was dashing off to see a game of tennis. And as Charles lived about five hundred years ago, it is obvious there is nothing new about tennis. Hippocrates, the Greek physician, was playing chess about four hundred years before Christ was born and is supposed to have said that it was a good cure for stomach trouble. And bingo, we are assured, was thought of by a nobleman in Genoa in the 16th century.

Outdoor games began with the discovery that hitting a ball with a stick could be fun. Nobody knows when the first ball was made, although they were used at the time when Troy was a flourishing city in Asia Minor in ancient times; and the Anglo-Saxons played a game called hand ball. Long ago, in England, a pig's bladder, filled with air, was used as a football, but the game was frowned upon because it interfered with archery practice.

The idea of hitting a ball with a stick must have arrived in very early times, and from it developed hockey, hurling, cricket, golf and other such games. One of Britain's oldest sports is bowls. As the Southampton Bowling Club had been founded in 1299, the game was an old one by the time Sir Francis Drake played it on Plymouth Hoe in 1588, before setting sail to defeat the Spanish Armada.

Lawn tennis is an offshoot of a similar indoor game called real tennis, which may have originated in the 10th or 11th century. Henry VII is known to have played it and his son, Henry VIII, built a court at Hampton Court Palace in 1530.

Golf enthusiasts have a royal precedent in Prince Henry, the eldest son of James I, who is said to have been a good player.

Nobody is certain when the first ball was made but its discovery has led to the creation of a large number of games.

Lawn tennis is based upon real tennis (above), a very old game which may have originated in the 10th or 11th centuries. Henry VII is known to have played and his son, Henry VIII built a court at Hampton Court Palace in 1520.

Prince Henry, the eldest son of James 1, was adept at golf (above). A similar game must have been played long before this for, in the great east window of Gloucester Cathedral, a 14th century golfer is depicted in stained glass. Some people claim that this figure represents a hockey player, but another player is actually shown "putting" in an early 16th century manuscript in the British Museum. Cricket (left) developed from the old club and ball games of the past. Spelled "crickett", it was first mentioned in the 16th century.

A similar game must have been played long before his time, however, for in the great east window of Gloucester Cathedral there is a 14th century golfer depicted in stained glass. And there is a 16th century manuscript in the British Museum showing a golfer.

Britain's great summer sport of cricket has grown from the old club and ball games of the past. Spelt "crickett", it is found in the 16th century corporation records of Guildford, Surrey. Originally, the wickets were holes in the ground. Then two stumps and a single bail were used and, in 1775, a third stump was added. Under-arm bowling was the rule until 1864 when over-arm bowling took its place.

Those who take their pleasures less energetically also play games steeped in antiquity. Chess is one of the oldest and probably originated in India, from where it spread, being brought to Europe by the Arabs. King Canute was said to

have played a game very like modern chess. Sometimes tempers flared when the rivalry was keen. William the Conqueror, when a boy, is said to have hit the king of France's son over the head with a chess board and as a result was sent back home to Normandy in disgrace.

Some indoor games have their origin in ancient battle exercises. Darts, for example, developed from spear throwing. The Pilgrim Fathers are said to have played darts to pass the time as they sailed across the Atlantic in 1620 in the ship, "Mayflower". But the modern game dates only from around the 1920s, when the rules were laid down by a committee of licensed victuallers.

A game that was very popular with the English nobility was shuffle-board. It was like our shove-halfpenny, only the board was a table up to thirty feet long, along which weights were slid. Nowadays, shuffle-board is played as a deck game aboard ocean liners, although the rules have changed a little.

Billiards was popular in the 18th century, being made fashionable by Louis XIV of France who played it after every

Henry VIII was a keen tennis player and had built, at Hampton Court Palace, a court for the use of himself and his guests. Visitors to the palace can still see these royal courts.

Knucklebones (top) was played thousands of years ago in Babylonia. Even whipping tops (above) date from this time. In fact, toys and games change very slowly. Boys used to blow soap bubbles through straws. After this they used clay pipes, (right) and today bubbles are still blown by children.

meal for exercise. Another game that was played by fashionable gentry in those days was battledore and shuttlecock. It was like badminton without a net—the bat being called a battledore— and it could really only be played indoors because the feathered shuttlecock was blown about in any wind. When badminton was devised, during the 1860s at Badminton Hall, battledore and shuttlecock went out of favour almost at once.

Card games have always been popular, but seldom so much as they were in the 19th century when whist clubs sprang up throughout London and became the centres of fashionable and political life. Playing cards were probably invented in China and reached England in the Middle Ages. The markings changed over the centuries, but today's playing cards with their hearts, clubs, diamonds and spades were developed in France 400 years ago. They have hardly changed since.

Even more deeply rooted in the past are many children's games which are as old as history itself. We know that knucklebones or five stones was played four thousand years ago in Babylonia, and it was still being played in Greece sixteen hundred years later. Even today, five-stones are played by children all over Europe.

A famous Babylonian carving, rescued from the dust of thousands of years, shows children playing with a whipping top just like they do today. In fact, toys and games change very slowly. Boys used to blow soap bubbles through straws, and when clay pipes came into being they made bubbles with these. In the 15th century, windmills on sticks were made of paper; today they are made of plastic. And kites, which have been flown in China for thousands of years, were very much the same in Europe three centuries ago as they are today.

It just goes to show that, despite the age of invention in which we live, when we find a good thing we keep it. If it were otherwise, all the pastimes from the past could not have survived to delight us today, as they will undoubtedly remain to delight our descendants in the far distant future.

PRINCE·WITH·A·PURPOSE·

The dockers were becoming desperate. To get work heaving ballast into empty holds to make ships steady they had to drink at certain riverside taverns; and drink, and drink, and drink, or else they got no work from the men running the wharves. The consequence was that nearly all their pitiable earnings were used up, while at the same time their health was undermined.

So in despair they wrote to the Master of Trinity House, honorary head of the great organisation for the benefit of shipping, who at that time happened to be the Prince Consort, Albert, husband of Queen Victoria. Always a notable champion of the working man, he was

Prince Albert survived early unpopularity to become a hero to most of the British people.

appalled by this sordid story of corruption and took instant action to stop the racket.

When Albert died, the ballast heavers wrote to his inconsolable widow to tell her how he had saved them. "We got no help until we sent our appeal to your late Royal Consort . . . At once our wrongs were redressed and the system that had ruined us swept away."

It was these workers who first christened the Prince

"Albert the Good" and the name stuck.

Perhaps some readers will now be bracing themselves for a sermon about a saint. They should resist the temptation, for the story of how Albert, the despised German princeling, won the hearts of the British, is a fine one. Most of the British would be more accurate, for the majority of the aristocracy never ceased to dislike him. Instead of being "one of them," the "dashed" foreigner preferred professional people, scientists, thinkers, musicians, even actors to their company, and actually wanted to better the lot of the poor. Even when he showed he could ride with the best of them to hounds, braving every obstacle, they still looked down on him, though they could hardly call him a coward. Only those lords who worked with him realised his worth in the end. Even the belligerent Lord Palmerston whose favourite form of diplomacy when British interests were threatened, was "Send a gunboat!", came to admire his character and brains, and wept when he died.

Albert was born in 1819, the younger son of the Duke of Saxe-Coburg, a small German kingdom at a time when Germany was still divided into many principalities. He married the lively young Queen Victoria when he was 21 and began a long struggle to do his duty for the good of his wife's people. The Queen was madly in love with him, but he had to struggle to assert his authority, first in the home, then outside it, for he had no official position. Wanting to better the nation, he could not sit in on meetings between Victoria and her ministers, but once they realised his quick brain and devotion to duty, his advice was constantly sought and his thoughts considered and often acted upon. Shy, and no courtier—though utterly courteous—he survived early unpopularity and, later, fatuous rumours in times of crisis that he was a foreign spy. His fine character made those who knew him feel better every time they met him, but, more important in the wider sense, he was no mere palace-bound prince. The Great Exhibition of 1851, though not his idea, only happened because he saw the marvellous scheme through despite all obstacles, which included fears of criminals converging on London, markets flooded with cheap goods and, from Church extremists, fears that the vengeance of the Almighty would sweep down on so arrogant a scheme.

As it was, the Exhibition was a triumph for the world's first industrial power and for the arts and crafts of the world in general, for many nations contributed exhibits and goods to the vast display. As for Albert, his adoring wife claimed that "All is owing to Albert—All to him," which, allowing for wifely exaggeration, was basically true.

This excellent man, when chairing a meeting of the Society for Improving the Condition of the Working Classes, publicly ticked off what are called today the bosses for not understanding and helping their workers. He demanded shorter working hours, proper education for the poor, and better housing for them. And he and his family were eminently respectable, a very important factor in popularising the Monarchy, which had been dragged into disrepute by earlier scandals of Victoria's ancestors and "wicked uncles". Today, Victorian respectability is often condemned as hypocritical, but that was not Albert's fault. His character was admirable in every way except one in which his virtue became a vice.

This was in his treatment of his eldest son, Bertie. later Edward VII. So protective was he, so fearful that the boy might be exposed to temptations of any kind, that the poor young prince had no friends of his own age, and a kindly tutor was removed because Bertie's work was

not good enough, and a stern disciplinarian put in his place. Albert meant well—he always did—but in this case he blundered. Not suprisingly, the Prince of Wales later became so fond of enjoying himself that his mother, now without her Albert, was in a constant state of distress about him.

Long before this, Albert and Victoria had endured a number of assassination attempts, the most dramatic being in 1840 only a few yards from Buckingham Palace —shades of Princess Anne in 1974—when they were riding in a small four-horse carriage. A man was leaning against a railing of Green Park and took a shot at the couple. The carriage stopped and Albert put his arm around his wife, then saw that the man had a pistol in each hand. He took aim, a pistol resting on his arm, and fired again, but missed, and the carriage drove on. The country rejoiced at the escape and that incident marked the beginning of stirrings of popularity for the Prince. In 1857 his position was finally and properly acknowledged when he was made

The Great Exhibition of 1851 was a triumph for British industry and for Prince Albert who had masterminded it through all its stages, despite much opposition.

Prince Consort.

But his greatest achievement was his last. It happened just before he died of typhoid in 1861, soon after the American Civil War had broken out. The Southern States, or the Confederacy, had split from the rest of the Union over the linked questions of states' rights and and slavery (many Southerners were slave-owners). The Confederate government sent envoys across the Atlantic to Britain and France, whose governments tended to side with the South, even though workers sided with the Union cause. An American warship stopped the British ship *Trent*, and took off the two envoys and their two secretaries, a flagrant breach of neutrality and international law. If there had been a trans-atlantic telegraph at that date, Britain and the U.S.A. might have gone to war, which would have been a catastrophe. As it was, the Foreign Secretary, Earl Russell, wrote a dispatch so strongly worded that it would probably have led to war anyway. The prince studied the letter and toned it down to become a polite request for the four to be released and a suitable apology made. The American Government, soothed by the note, did just what was asked. Albert rewrote the letter and showed it to Victoria on the morning of December 1. Palmerston, the Prime Minister, accepted the alterations and the crisis was soon to be over. But by the time it was, Albert had died, on December 14. The country's loss was as great as Victoria's if different, for Albert was still young, with many years of service, it had seemed, before him. He may not have been the greatest of the eminent Victorians but by any known standard he was the most admirable man among them.

TO GET TO THE OTHER SIDE...

Napoleon thought it was a good idea—and who can blame him? A tunnel under the English Channel carrying road traffic between Britain and France would be good for trade between the two countries separated by only 21 miles of water. As Emperor of France, he had everything to gain and nothing to lose from such a project.

But the British people did not share his enthusiasm for this scheme. For centuries, they had felt secure behind the strip of water that flowed between them and the continent of Europe. And Napoleon's ambitions for greater and greater power were well known. It would be easy for him to march his troops through the tunnel and add Britain to his list of conquests, they thought. And so Napoleon's proposals which he had made to the British ambassador at the beginning of the 19th century were turned down.

They were raised again in 1876, when Britain and France finally came to an agreement to link their two countries with a tunnel. They even went so far as to dig experimental tunnels for 2,000 yards on either side. But the work was stopped in 1882, probably because of Britain's fears about the use an invader could make of the tunnel.

British Rail ferries ply regularly across the channel, taking thousands of passengers and their cars across this narrow strip of water which separates the British from their neighbours.

The Channel has been conquered by air and sea — by balloons, planes and all kinds of boats and by powerful swimmers. But the dream of such men as Napoleon Bonaparte that a tunnel would one day link England and France has not so far been realized.

The idea came up again in 1914, but was stopped because the First World War broke out in that year. Now, it is being talked about again and the chances that it may at least be built are more rosy. No longer does Britain fear invasion from the continent, because modern warfare has produced more effective ways of subduing an enemy, principally by air attacks.

When the tunnel is built, we may be able to board a train in Britain and go straight to our destination on the continent. We shall then have an advantage over today's cross-channel trippers who have a choice of hopping there by air, going by fast luxury steamers, train and car

ferries, or making exciting, noisy dashes above the waves by hovercraft.

Their great-grandparents also had a choice, and they loved Channel trips. But how different were conditions in their day!

Excursions to the Continent multiplied when the railways reached Dover and Folkestone. There were three rival rail systems: the South Eastern: the London, Chatham and Dover Railway, and the South Eastern and Chatham. Competition between them was intense.

Folkestone Harbour was completed by the South Eastern Railway in 1842, and within a year the first steamer was sailing for Boulogne. Soon 100,000 passengers were making the trip yearly among them Queen Victoria, who chose that route when on her way to the French Riviera.

An early advertisement of the South-Eastern and Chatham Railway tells of "Royal Mail Express Services via Dover-Calais and Folkestone-Boulogne." The sea passage to Calais took between 65 and 75 minutes; that to Boulogne from 80 to 100 minutes, with five services in each direction daily. "London and Paris in less than $7\frac{1}{2}$ hours" was the claim.

A picture painted by Howard Geach in about 1865 is entitled *The Boat Train, South Eastern Railway, Dover Harbour*. The engine, black, red and green, has a brassbound funnel. Coaches are "Wellington brown," with very pale salmon pink upper panels. Waves are washing over the track as the train steams off the Admiralty Pier.

Alternatively, the passengers of those days could, if they liked, choose the London, Chatham and Dover Railway, running from Dover Harbour Station, to Victoria. A glimpse of this may be seen in the background of the

same painting.

In those days, boats approaching harbour signalled the numbers of passengers carried. Each of a number of balls on the foremast indicated 100 passengers; a ball on the mainmast meant 20; a flag on the foremast indicated 50 and one on the mainmast 25. A ball at the peak, over the ensign, signified 10.

The early paddle-steamers were quite small—300 tons gross or less. Their speed was between 11 and 12 knots.

A day return-trip between Dover and Calais cost 15s. 6d. ($77\frac{1}{2}$p), but many holidaymakers made a circular tour by way of Dover-Calais-Boulogne-Folkestone-Dover, which had to be completed within eight days.

"On a fine, calm day," says an old guide-book "or when a favourable breeze enables a sail or two to be carried to steady the boat, the passage is full of enjoyment."

But who could guarantee a fine, calm day? Then, as now, the Channel could cause travellers plenty of discomfort, and designers were always trying out new ideas.

Attempts to defeat Channel sickness produced some strange vessels. One, the *Castalia*, was a sort of glorified catamaran. She had two half-hulls, with a pair of paddle wheels one behind the other between them. She also had four funnels, four bows and four rudders. Not surprisingly, she was not a good sea-boat, and had difficulty in making ten knots. She was soon dropped.

Another ambitious freak was the *Bessemer*. Double-ended, with four paddles and two

Two views of a trip to
France in Victorian times,
as seen by a contemporary
cartoonist.

funnels, this vessel was supposed to protect
her passengers from sea sickness by accommo-
dating them in a suspended saloon amidships.
She rode heavy seas well on a trial run, then
collided with a pier and smashed a paddle. She
also damaged a pier on her maiden voyage.
After a while, she was sold for scrap.

But nothing could discourage the travellers,
whose numbers increased by day and by night.
Charles Dickens gives a vivid picture of a night
crossing in his *The Uncommercial Traveller*,
describing the arrival of the night mail at Dover
as follows:

"A screech, a bell, and two red eyes come
gliding down the Admiralty Pier with a smooth-

ness of motion rendered more smooth by the
heaving of the boat. The sea makes noises
against the pier as if several hippoppotami were
tapping at it."

In those days, words of command were constantly being shouted: "Stand by below!"
"Half a turn ahead!" "Half speed!" "Port!"
"Go on!", and so on. Dickens lists them faith-
fully; notes the "hiccuppy" South Foreland
lights; the ever-present stench of oil; notes the
progress of stewards examining tickets by the light
of bull's-eye lanterns as they warn passengers
that it is going to be "a rough night tonight."

Calais is reached at last, and passengers go
their various ways, as they still do today.

Modern hovercraft have
cut the time for crossing
the channel to half an hour.

And if the weather is too
rough for these small one
man hovercraft they can
always tuck themselves inside one of their bigger
brothers for the trip.

DRAKE~Hero or Villain?

As the night wore on the dying sailor's delirium began to abate and he lay quietly in his bunk. At the height of his fever he had ordered that his armour should be put on him so that he might die like a soldier, which was right and proper, for the stocky bearded Devon man, Sir Francis Drake, the greatest seaman of his age, had also achieved prodigies with his sword, leading his men in daring land battles in the towns and jungles of Spanish America.

But those days were past. This last expedition to the fabulous Spanish Main, begun in 1595, had been dogged by ill fortune, not least the death of his great kinsman, Sir John Hawkins, another of Elizabeth I's sea-dogs, and one of the greatest of them. Now "El Draque", as the Spaniards called him, whose very name was used by Spanish mothers to frighten their children into being good, was dying too. On January 28, 1596, off Porto Bello his adventures ended, and the next day, the Master Thief of the Unknown World, as one Spaniard had half-admiringly christened him, vanished into the water in a lead coffin as sad trumpets blared and cannon blazed.

That is the heroic view of Drake and a true one. But there is another side to the story. He has been called a pirate, a cruel man, greedy for spoil, a sailor who disobeyed orders, who was mixed up in the early history of the infamous slave trade, which transported blacks to a life of misery in the West Indies and America. True, he, more than anyone else, had defeated the mighty Spanish Armada in 1588, but for years before that he had waged war on Spain when the two countries were still officially at peace. Was he then a villainous adventurer, or a man worthy to be one of the supreme national heroes of the English and the other British to this day?

Villainous is far too strong a word, but he does seem to have been half hero, half rogue. Yet only by today's standards. Not everyone liked him in his own day, but to the people of England he was their special hero. A whole book could scarcely do justice to his amazing career, so only some highlights of it and controversies can be touched on here.

Born around 1642 in Devon, he was a seaman before his teens, and by the time he was 20 he was sailing with Hawkins to Guinea and the Spanish Main as a 3rd officer. Hawkins was partly concerned with carrying slaves across the Atlantic. Repugnant as this seems to us today, most leading figures in Elizabethan times from the Queen downwards were involved, and most European countries, while thousands of Christian slaves languished in northern Africa. It was not a question of colour: slaves were of all colours. We rightly condemn it, but it is fatuous to write off whole peoples because of it, let alone Drake. The 20th century has enough on its conscience and the Elizabethans thought differently to us.

Drake was soon fiercely anti-Spanish, but stories of his cruelty are sheer myth and Spanish propaganda. On one expedition he and Hawkins were treacherously attacked, which helped increase his enmity, and as a patriot and a Protestant at a time when Spain was the great enemy and the world's greatest power—because of the wealth of her American empire—it was hardly likely

On his great voyage round the world, Drake plundered the Spanish ruthlessly but did not kill a single Spaniard.

that an English sailor would love Spain, especially as the Spaniards treated prisoners so harshly. As "heretics", English sailors were often tortured, burnt, killed outright or condemned to the living death of slavery in the galleys. Drake, however, spared prisoners as a rule, often setting them free. On his great voyage around the world he plundered the Spaniards hugely but did not kill a single one of them. So much for his cruelty.

By modern standards he was a pirate, just as his enemies were, but it is more accurate to think of him waging an endless guerilla war against Spain, while lining his own pockets, and his backers' coffers. They often included the Queen.

Drake's sailors adored him. A pushing, self-made man, liable to blaze with anger, he collected his share of enemies, but they were never his own men. On his first solo expedition in 1572, they refused the chance of plundering Nombre de Dios because he was so badly wounded. They were to make up for it, for later, with their Cimarron allies, who were partly escaped slaves, partly Indians, they ambushed a mule train and ran off with a fortune in silver and gold, worth about £600,000 in today's terms. Meanwhile, from the top of a high tree in the Isthmus of Panama, Drake had seen the Pacific and sworn he would sail an English ship upon it.

After that expedition Drake was a famous and wealthy man. His voyage around the world (1577-80) made him an immortal. Only his ship, the *Pelican* re-christened *The Golden Hind*, survived the voyage, two others being broken up for firewood because they were unseaworthy, one sinking with all hands, and another returning home. Yet Drake brought back plunder worth £18 million in

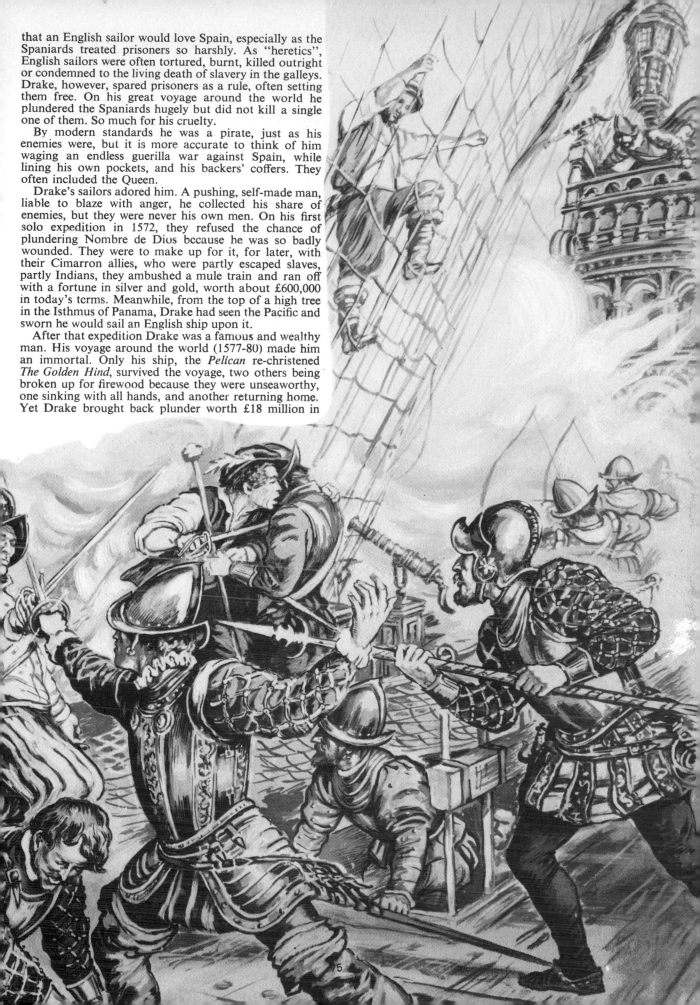

today's terms, enough to pay for the war against the Armada twice over.

On the voyage he had to execute a gentleman adventurer named Thomas Doughty for mutinous conduct. Arguments still rage over this, especially among people who have never commanded a desperate, or, indeed, any venture. It led to a famous statement. "Gentlemen" could be menaces aboard ship and Drake, the self-made man, said: "My masters, I must have the gentleman to haul and draw with the mariner, and the mariner with the gentleman. What, let us show ourselves all to be of one company!"

Drake was knighted by Elizabeth after the voyage, to the fury of an already furious Spain. But many Catholic rulers half admired the dashing Drake, even if he was an English devil and a heretic.

Now undeclared war was waged, with the Queen trying for peace as was her duty, for England was surrounded by enemies and not rich, and Drake doing his duty, which culminated in almost wiping out the Spanish fleet in Cadiz harbour in 1587: "singeing the King of Spain's beard", as Drake called it. But the next year the Armada came, and Drake, second-in-command to Lord Howard of Effingham, was the master-mind—along with the weather—which defeated it. He took time off in the middle of the battle to capture a prize, or so his enemies alleged, but so did Lord Howard. Men combined business with pleasure then, and it is useless judging a navy consisting mainly of privateers by the standards of the later Royal Navy. And if Drake had had his way, the Armada would never have sailed: he would have singed the King's beard again.

After the Armada, apart from one attack on the Spanish and Portuguese coasts, which destroyed much shipping but foundered from sickness and lack of provisions, Drake led a peaceful existence. He became Plymouth's M.P. and gave the town its first proper water supply. When the new channel carrying the water was opened, Drake rode along it to the sound of trumpets, a gesture typically Elizabethan and typical of Drake. Then came the last fatal voyage and Drake died in the

Drake's sailors ambushed a mule train and ran off with a fortune in silver and gold.

very waters where he had first made his name.

Because of him and his companions, England, beset by enemies, remained secure and became prosperous. True, she had a careful, brilliant Queen and notable statesmen, but the sailors saved her. Like the poets and playwrights, the adventurers and explorers they were that magic word "Elizabethans". The age is remembered as the Age of Elizabeth, of Shakespeare—and of Drake.

Queen Elizabeth knighted Drake to the fury of Spain whose riches he had plundered.

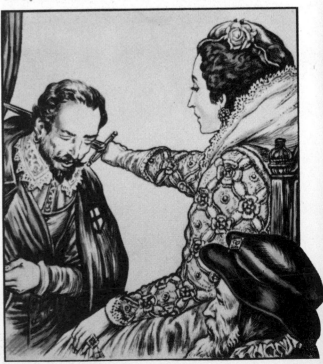

REVOLUTION!

Tsar Nicholas II and his family (above) whose subjects endured lives of grovelling humility (below).

77

Two hundred thousand men, women and children swarmed through the snowbound streets of St. Petersburgh, the capital of Russia, and now named Leningrad. Many carried pictures of the Tsar and sang "God save the Tsar" as they walked along.

Their leader was a gentle, black-bearded priest named Father Gapon, a young man of striking looks and great piety. Father Gapon held a letter which he hoped to hand to the Tsar while the crowd waited outside his palace. It was a petition for an improvement in the long hours of work which people had to endure in abysmal conditions for treacherously low pay.

Father Gapon intended it to be a peaceful demonstration, but something like panic seems to have seized the police and the military who were guarding the palace. They called upon the crowd to halt, but the people were determined to present their petition to the Tsar.

When the procession failed to halt, the soldiers opened fire. They fired from close range straight into a screaming wall of people who could do nothing to avoid the massacre. More than five hundred were killed and thousands wounded. The blood of the victims dyed the snows red. For history, January 22, 1905, has come to be known as Bloody Sunday.

Nothing now could hold back the violence that had been seething in Russia during the reign of Tsar Nicholas. A member of the Romanov family, Nicholas had been ruling Russia for more than ten years. He was the head of a vast country stretching across one-sixth of the world's land surface. Yet, despite its forests, its goldfields, its oil wells and fertile plains, Russia was living in the Middle Ages.

A small but ruthless group of aristocrats ruled the land. The Tsar himself had estates the size of France. The peasants scratched a living from the soil in the primitive fashion of feudal serfs, keeping their masters fabulously rich while they and their families often starved.

Most of Russia's factories, power stations and coal mines were owned by foreign companies. Workers in them endur dreadful conditions, toiling often for twelve or fourteen hours day for seven days a week. Children went to the factories wi their mothers. There were few schools and few people cou read or write.

This was Russia in 1905, a fuse smouldering with disconten and soon now the spark was to reach the powderbowl o revolution.

The government founded, as a safety valve, a society at which working men could air their grumbles, but the police made sure that its meetings were conducted with a due show of loyalty towards the Tsar. They even supported Father Gapon as the workers' leader.

After Bloody Sunday, Father Gapon wrote to the Tsar, "Let all the blood that has to be shed fall upon you and those like you."

Strikes and terrorism broke out in the cities. In the Black Sea, the crew of the battleship Potemkin mutinied. The revolution was crushed. The Tsar survived. But the fire of revolt ran underground, gathering heat for an eruption that would yet shake the world.

After the revolution, the Tsar was forced to yield some of his power. He founded the Duma, Russia's first parliament. But still discontent grew and in April, 1912, there came an atrocity to revive memories of the Bloody Sunday massacre of 1905. Workers in the Lena goldfields refused to endure their feudal conditions any more. When they protested, the police shot them down.

News of the massacre spread swiftly and the tempo of unrest quickened. Then, in 1914, Russia was caught up in the First World War. Even those most critical of the Tsar supported him as he urged his armies into an offensive against Germany.

But the enthusiasm was short-lived. Russia's armies were as impoverished as her people, and often there was only one rifle between ten men. Soon, the ammunition had almost run out. Soldiers began to desert in thousands and strikes broke out.

When the Tsar sent the Russian army to fight the Germans in 1914 the nation supported him. But soon discontent spread among the troops. Ammunition was in short supply and the troops were badly armed. Soon men began to defy their officers and desert their posts.

A huge crowd greeted Lenin's return to Petrograd. But the people were soon shocked to silence by what he had to say.

In March, 1917, apparently unaware of his unpopularity, the Tsar left Petrograd (as St. Petersburgh had since been renamed) for his military headquarters, unaware that he was leaving his capital for the last time.

Meanwhile, the angry fire of revolt was running through Petrograd. Starving workers demanded bread and women carried banners saying, "End the War". As the mob surged towards the Tsar's palace, the military governor, General Khabalov, ordered his soldiers to shoot. They raised their rifles—and fired harmlessly into the air. The revolt was spreading to the army too.

Another army group was called into action. They shot directly into the crowd, killing sixty and driving the rest berserk. Police stations were looted, burned, destroyed. Jails were broken open and prisoners—thieves, murderers and revolutionaries—set free.

After this revolution, a new government was formed. But it soon became clear that this government had no intention of ending the war.

Soon defiant voices were heard all over the country as workers, soldiers and peasants banded together in groups called Soviets. Most powerful of these was the Petrograd Soviet, which turned against the government, urging the armies to do no more than defend their country against Germany so that Russia's minister might seek peace.

One man was missing from Russia at this time, a dynamic man of action who was soon to set the murmurs of discontent boiling again into revolution. His name was Vladimir Ilyich Ulyanov, known to the world as Lenin. For twenty years, he had been in and out of exile, using every minute of his time in Siberia, London and Switzerland to weave the fabric of revolt.

In 1917, Lenin was in Switzerland, but in close touch with his homeland. Now he saw his chance and returned to Russia, arriving in Petrograd on April 16 to a tumultuous welcome. But the crowd was soon shocked to silence when he told them that their revolution was only half a revolution. The Soviets—the

council of soldiers, workers and peasants—were the key to power. They must take control of the government. The war must be ended. For the peasants there must be land; for the people bread and peace.

For six months, Lenin drove his Bolsheviks mercilessly, preparing to seize power. Everywhere he held meetings, captivating huge audiences with his oratory. In Leon Trotsky, president of the Petrograd Soviet, Lenin found a powerful ally, and the pair made their plans together.

The rising was fixed for November 7, 1917 and within that day, the Soviets had taken power. The Russian government melted away, almost without resistance.

Soon, Lenin formed a new Bolshevik government. He sent Trotsky to sign a peace treaty with the Germans, obtaining the harshest of terms. But there was still no peace for their racked and tortured country. So far, the revolution had brought little bloodshed. Now, as armies of counter-revolutionaries began to invade Russia, the blood began to flow. Tsar Nicholas and his family were murdered.

Everywhere, the Bolshevik armies retreated, but they fought on. By 1920, Lenin had won—and faced a new battle against poverty, famine, illiteracy and disease. Before he could win, his life ran out. On January 21, 1924, he died.

Lenin was succeeded by Joseph Stalin who used his position to make himself dictator of Russia and, by a series of five year plans, developed industry, agriculture and education in an effort to bring his country forward from the Middle Ages to the twentieth century.

But his rule was extremely harsh and, after his death in 1953, Stalin was succeeded by other rulers who have attempted to establish a more moderate rule.

Today, Russia is a world power—a far cry from the tattered, strife-torn nation that existed in the unhappy days of the Tsars.

HISTORY QUIZ

Now that you have read the articles in our history section, see if you can answer the questions about them below.

(Turn to the back of the book for the answers.)

1. Which royal consort was the mastermind behind Britain's Great Exhibition of 1851?

2. Who was the dictator who disapproved of the successes gained by black athletes in the 1936 Olympic Games?

3. Why was Fred Lorz disqualified in the marathon race at the Olympic Games of 1904?

4. What are the names of the cities on which atomic bombs were dropped in 1945, near the end of the Second World War?

5. Some Japanese pilots deliberately crashed their planes on enemy ships. What were these pilots called in Japanese?

6. Which royal family was ruling Britain at the end of the 17th century?

7. In 1670, when a yeoman was selected to serve in the militia, how was his military service performed?

8. What other problems had beset Britain at the time of the Dutch war in 1666?

9. How many ships did the British fleet lose in its four day battle with the Dutch?

10. Charles VIII of France hit his head as he was dashing off to see a game. What sport was he going to watch?

11. What use was made of a pig's bladder filled with air long ago in England?

12. What game, popular today, is supposed to have been invented by a Genoese nobleman in the 16th century?

13. To what game does an English stately home give its name?

14. Who was the King who gave England its name and when did he come to power?

15. At whose court in France did this king learn the art of war?

16. What is the name of the dyke which formed a boundary between Wales and England?

17. In what year did Lenin return to Russia and inspire his people in their revolution?

18. Who ruled Russia as a harsh dictator between 1924 and 1953?

19. What did Napoleon regard as an ideal way of crossing the English Channel?

20. Which famous English novelist described a trip by sea across the English Channel in his book, "The Uncommercial Traveller?"

WILDLIFE WONDERLAND

Nature

In the high canopy live the larger birds. Predators, such as the tawny owl, hobby, sparrow-hawk; plant-eaters like the wood pigeon, and other birds including magpies, jackdaws, jays, and carrion crows.

Magpie

Carrion Crow

A casual onlooker can walk through a wood and see only trees and plants. But the peace and tranquility of a wood can deceive the eyes and ears, for a closer look can reveal a wealth of wild life activity which often remains concealed from view when the observer does not know what to look for.

To understand the workings of wild-life in a woodland environment, it is important to remember that it consists of a highly complex web of relationships by which thousands of plants and animals live together. The behaviour and activities of one inhabitant of the wood can affect every other

The canopy of a wood in Britain usually stretches up to about 60 feet. The canopy of an oak wood is teeming with insect life, and that of a sycamore wood contains a great variety of insects where aphids (plant lice) attract spiders and the larvae of hoverflies and ladybirds.

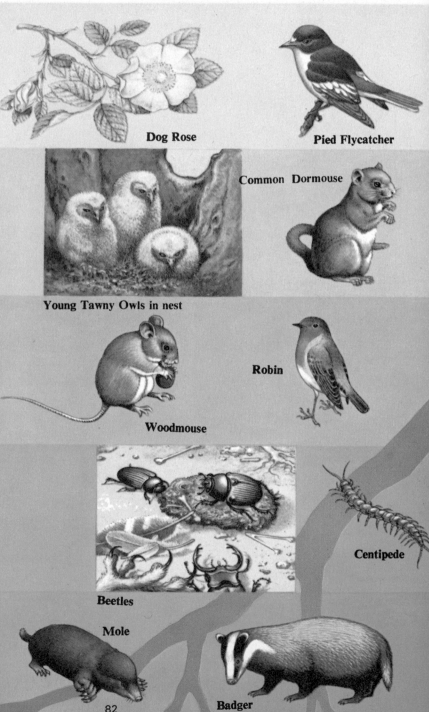

Dog Rose

Pied Flycatcher

The layer which goes up to about six feet above the ground is called the field layer. Here, flowering plants flourish, and animals feed on plant tissues, pollen and fruits. Many types of birds feed, nest and shelter in the field layer and small mammals like the dormouse belong to this layer.

Common Dormouse

Young Tawny Owls in nest

The surface of the ground, with its vegetation covering of mosses, lichen and low-growing plants, contains a large variety of animals. Grasshoppers, spiders, ants, voles mice and shrews are the inhabitants of this layer. The chiffchaff and willow warbler nest on the ground but fly up to the conapy to live and feed.

Robin

Woodmouse

The next layer, the topsoil, is rich in decomposing organisms which live on dead and decaying plants and animals. Earthworms, moth caterpillars, the larvae of flies, beetles, as well as fungi and bacteria, all help to decompose dead material and contribute to the growth of new plants in the wood.

Centipede

Beetles

The lowest layer of the wood is the subsoil where rabbits and badgers dig their burrows and which consists of the dead leaves of trees and plants. Earthworms sometimes descend to this level from the layer above.

Mole

Badger

Wood Pigeon

Tawny Owl
roosting

Sparrow Hawk

living thing around it. The creatures and plants which live in a wood fall into two main kinds; the producers and the consumers. The producers are the plants, while the consumers are first, the plant-eating animals, above them their predators; and above these *their* predators, and so on. In addition to these are the decomposers. such as fungi and bacteria whose job it is to break down dead animal and plant material and return them to the soil to further plant growth.

There are several distinct layers in a wood which you can see from the beautiful illustration on this page.

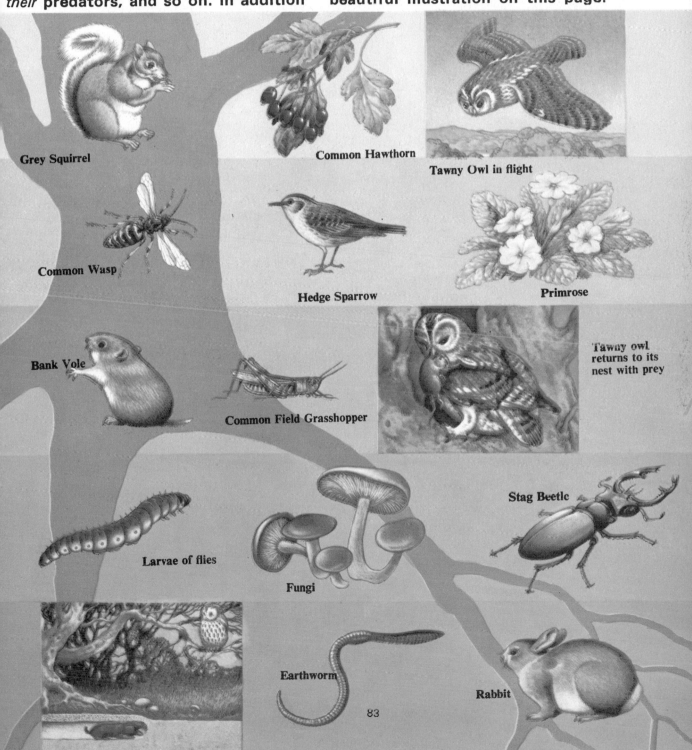

Grey Squirrel

Common Hawthorn

Tawny Owl in flight

Common Wasp

Hedge Sparrow

Primrose

Bank Vole

Common Field Grasshopper

Tawny owl returns to its nest with prey

Larvae of flies

Fungi

Stag Beetle

Earthworm

Rabbit

Royal Beasts of Britain

For hundreds of years the wild deer of Britain have been regarded as the Royal beasts of the chase, but during the last two centuries these beautiful creatures have been protected from the huntsman. Over the years Britain's two native deer were joined by five other members of the deer family.

Reindeer

Until the 12th century Reindeer were hunted Scotland. Then, they disappeared from the countr probably as a result of over-killing and of the cleari of forests where these creatures like to take refug In 1952 a Lapp farmer brought some of his Swedi herd to the Cairngorms and since then, their numb has increased to 1000.

Chinese Water Deer

The Chinese Water Deer is only 18 inches high and has lived wild in Britain since one escaped from a zoo. Neither the male or the female has antlers, but the buck has large upper canines which protrude from its mouth like tusks. Since the 1940s this deer has spread to Huntingdonshire, Hampshire, the Chilterns and Oxfordshire. It is one of the most attractive of the wild animals of Britain.

The Sika

The Sika resembles the Red Deer in body and th shape of its antlers. It was introduced into park from Japan during the 17th century and today live wild in Dorset, Hampshire, Lancashire and Easter Ireland. Its rutting season lasts from September t November and the female gives birth to one ca some time between the beginning of June and th end of July.

Red Deer

The Red Deer, together with the Roe Deer, is a native to Britain. It is four feet high at the shoulder and is Britain's largest wild animal. It lives on the open mountains and moorlands in Scotlands Cumberland and the West Country. The hind, or female, bears one calf a year after the rutting season, in April or May.

Roe Deer

The other British native deer, the Roe Deer is 2 feet high and, like the Red and Fallow Deer, is a royal beast of the chase, preserved for centuries for hunting by the king and his court. This deer now lives in Scotland, the Lake District, the southern counties and in East Anglia. The female often gives birth to twins.

Fallow Deer

It was probably the Romans who brought the Fallow Deer to Britain from Asia Minor, to use it as a decorative estate animal and beast of the chase. Fallow Deer prefer to live in dense woodland but enter gardens and fields to raid crops and vegetables. During the summer the bucks and does keep apart, then herd together during the rutting season in October.

Muntjac

The tiny Muntjac, which reaches 16 to 25 inches high, is a hump backed creature and easily recognisable. It has lived wild in Britain since one escaped from Woburn Park in 1890. Since then, it has spread to the Home Counties, southern counties and East Anglia. Most of them are probably of the Chinese race, and like the Chinese Water Deer, the buck has tusk-like canines.

Gilbert White (above) and one of the many creatures he observed in his village of Selbourne, the Fieldmouse (below).

THE NATURE EXPLORERS

It seemed a rather odd thing for the local curate to do, but the people of Selbourne were not at all perplexed at the sight of a clergyman taking off his cassock after the church service and dropping to his knees to peer intently at a patch of grass in the churchyard.

The men and women who lived in that tiny Hampshire village in the middle of the eighteenth century were quite accustomed to this sight and knew that the Reverend Gilbert White was making yet another of his observations about nature to add to his knowledge of the hobby he so passionately followed.

Gilbert White was born on July 18th, the eldest of eleven children. He was educated at a grammar school and at Oriel College, Oxford and as a young man developed a great love for the countryside. His interest in natural history led him to keep a journal which he began in 1751 when he started to study the plants and creatures which he found in his own garden. Then, with two friends, who were also keen naturalists, Thomas Pennant and Daines Barrington, White began a correspondence of letters over a period of 14 years describing his discoveries. It was these letters, forty four addressed to Pennant, and sixty six to Barrington, which formed the substance of the book which was to make White famous, *The Natural History and Antiquities of Selbourne*. The work, published in 1788, is today recognised as a classic of English literature.

George Montagu who gave the first adequate account of the natural history of the Dartford Warbler (below).

Charles Darwin, the most famous and brilliant of all the naturalists of the 18th and 19th centuries, made a detailed study of orchids (below).

Flowers, plants, seeds, worms, insects, fish, birds—every aspect of wild life in Selbourne was carefully and painstakingly studied by the amateur enthusiast who had no formal scientific qualification and yet was able to advance botanical knowledge in Britain more than any professional scientific work had ever done.

One naturalist who is less famous than he deserves to be is John Ray who died before Gilbert White was born. Ray has often been called the Father of English natural history and his influence on later naturalists like White was very great.

Ray was born in 1628 the son of a blacksmith in Essex. He became a fellow at Cambridge University and there wrote his first book which was published in 1660. This was a catalogue of plants found in the area of Cambridge and was a wonderful achievement in accurate and detailed description. Ten years later he published a catalogue of English plants and then began to work on a new system of classification on which later scientists were to build, and which led to the system of giving every living thing two Latin names. Ray's interest in plants and insects was a lifelong one, but he was not simply a botanist. He observed animals too, and his zoological works have been described as the basis of modern zoology.

George Montagu, who was born in 1751, was one of the most brilliant naturalists of the 18th and 19th centuries. Montagu was an acute and accurate observer and his *Ornithological Dictionary* published in 1802, is a classic of natural history, and it is for his study of birds that he is best remembered.

In 1800 he distinguished the Cirl Bunting from the Yellowhammer for the first time in Britain. He was the first to describe the beautiful Roseate Tern. It was also Montagu who gave the first adequate account of the natural history of the Dartford Warbler. Today his name is remembered in animals. The bird, Montagu's harrier, the fish Montagu's blenny and Montagu's sea snail are all named after this very important naturalist.

By far the most famous and most brilliant of all naturalists of the 18th and 19th centuries was Charles Darwin. He was born at Shrewsbury on February 12th, 1809, the grandson of Erasmus Darwin and of Josiah Wedgwood, on his mother's side. He was educated at Edinburgh University and at Cambridge where his study of biology really began. In 1831 he took his degree and through his Professor, J. S. Henslow, the botanist, Darwin received an invitation to join H.M.S *Beagle* as expedition naturalist. For the next five years the expeditionary ship sailed on its scientific survey of South American and Pacific waters, and it was during this time that Darwin began the field studies which were to form the basis of his theory of evolution which was to shatter the world.

In 1856 he began work on a treatise of his views and three years later his most famous book was published. In his *Origin of the Species* by *Means of Natural Selection*, Darwin put forward the idea that all plants and animals are descended from a few original forms of life. He noted that in any species many more individuals were born than survived. From this observation, he deducted that there must be a struggle for survival and that in this struggle only the creatures who are fittest will be the ones to survive. Since the environment was constantly changing, he continued, it followed that all living things must also change and re-adapt in order to survive.

On the first day of its publication, the 1,250 copies of the first edition of *The Origin of the Species* were completely sold out.

In 1871 Darwin published *The Descent of Man* in which he related human beings to the ancestors of the great apes. This book caused almost as much outrageous indignation than the previous book.

But it was his *Origin of the Species* which led to the systematic study of natural history not only in Britain but throughout the whole world. The devastating impact of Darwin's views was to turn the world upside down, and today his theory of ever-changing evolving life is a generally accepted truth.

John Ray is often called the Father of English natural history. He published a catalogue of plants in 1660. Below: the Darewort.

UNUSUAL BEASTS OF AFRICA

Across the grasslands, forests and woodlands of Africa roam some of the most curious-looking animals in the world.

These long-legged acrobats of the loris family are found in Southern and Eastern Africa. Also called galagos, bushbabies are tremendously fast movers and can make spectacular leaps from one branch to another among the trees where they live.

Bushbabies come out to feed when night falls, their enormous eyes and large ears being very useful during their nocturnal hunting expeditions.

The female bushbaby gives birth to one or two young which are left in the nest while the mother goes out to find food. Sometimes, she will carry her young by the scruff of their necks, or allow them to cling to her body as she leaps.

Apart from its most unusual-sounding name, the Brindled Gnu or Wildebeest also has a rather peculiar appearance. It stands about 52 inches high at the shoulder, has a blue-grey body and black hairs on its mane and tail.

There are two distinctive kinds. The black-bearded Blue Wildebeest inhabits southern Africa, while the White-bearded Gnu lives in East Africa.

The Brindled Gnu likes to live in herds of about twenty to fifty of its kind. They are very dependent on water and often have to travel long distances to find a water source. They rest during the middle of the day and graze and drink during the cooler hours.

This extremely ugly creature of tropical Africa is commonly found roaming across open woodlands. It has a barrel-shaped body, with a warty face, short legs and a long thin tail. The coat which covers its body can hardly be called fur, for it is only a thin, scraggly covering with a crest of long, coarse hair running along its back. The face of the male warthog is covered with un-attractive looking warts.

The most form-idable enemy of the warthog is the leopard, against which the female, or sow is most careful to protect her three or four young which are born every year.

The Maned Rat of East Africa is a rather odd-looking creature with its large back and white body and the long strip of upturned hairs down the middle of its back. When danger threatens these hairs stand on end forming a crest shape along the back.

Only very little is known about this unusual rodent. It inhabits the high-lands in the forest country and makes burrows in the sides of the steep valleys or at the bottom of trees. It leaves its home under the earth when the sky dark-ens and for most of the night wanders about in search of insects.

One of the strangest of all the animals in the world, the Aardvark or Earth Pig, roams across the grasslands of Africa just outside canopy forests.

Its long, pig-like snout is not the only peculiar feature of its appearance. It has a pair of long, donkey-like ears which . stand upright on the top of its head.

The Aardvark is a champion termite hunter and has well developed claws which enables it to dig quickly through termite mounds. These are picked up by means of the Aardvark's 12-inch, sticky tongue.

This spectacular looking creature has a highly conspicuous appearance like that of the American skunk Also called the Striped Weasel, the Zorilla of Africa has black fur under its body with a broad white stripe running along its back. Its large bushy tail is pure white, and across its face is another white band of fur.

It not only resembles the Striped Skunk of America in this way, but also has well developed glands which are capable of throwing out a foul-smelling liquid. Like the Skunk, the Zorilla uses this as a self defence mechanism when it is threatened with danger.

Danger At Sea

N ature red in tooth and claw" applies just as much to the inhabitants of the murky depths of the ocean as it does to creatures of the land The sea also has its 'tigers'.

Although the majority of fish are harmless and inoffensive there are some whose ferocity is unmatched by the fiercest of land animals.

Even the poisonous rattlesnake and scorpion have their counterparts under the sea and it is only in water that victims of aggression are killed with powerful electric shocks.

At the bottom of the deepest seas, known as the abyss, there is a nightmare world of perpetual darkness inhabited by the most fantastic creatures

The extrordinary-looking fish shown below, for example, has powerful poisonous spines The 'Scorpion' or 'Lion' Fish is about one foot long and striped, as you can see, like a zebra. Its pectoral and dorsal fins are extended into long ribbon-like strips and among its fins are eighteen poison spines which are used only in self-defence. This evil-looking creature shares its home with many strange, luminous fish with lures on top of their heads which hang over their gaping mouths to attract their prey, and others able to dislocate their jaws so that they can swallow fish three or four times their own size.

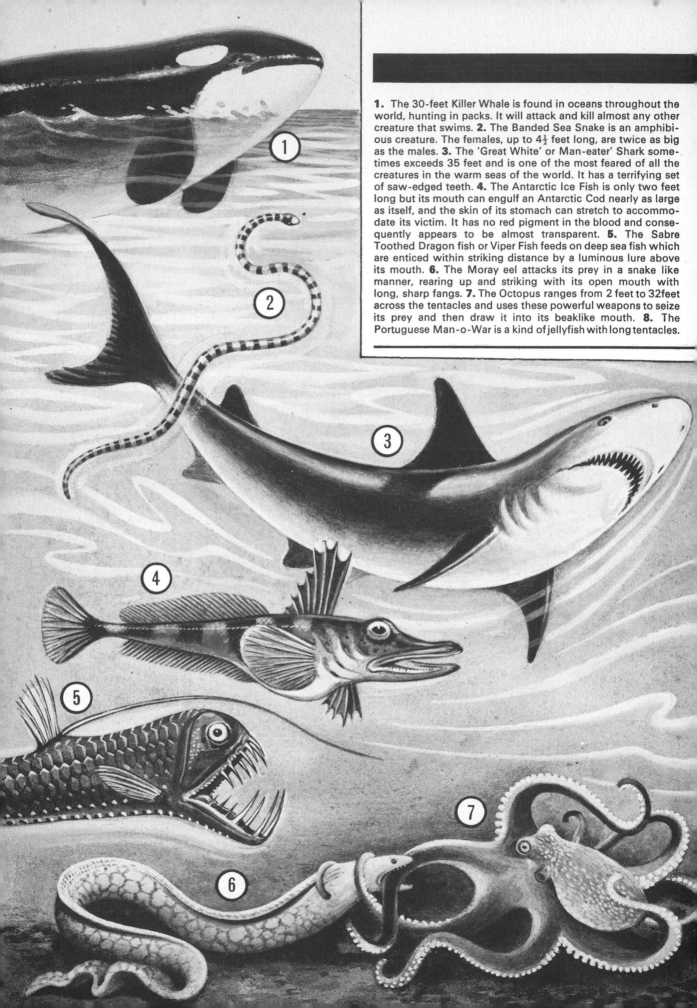

1. The 30-feet Killer Whale is found in oceans throughout the world, hunting in packs. It will attack and kill almost any other creature that swims. **2.** The Banded Sea Snake is an amphibious creature. The females, up to 4½ feet long, are twice as big as the males. **3.** The 'Great White' or Man-eater' Shark sometimes exceeds 35 feet and is one of the most feared of all the creatures in the warm seas of the world. It has a terrifying set of saw-edged teeth. **4.** The Antarctic Ice Fish is only two feet long but its mouth can engulf an Antarctic Cod nearly as large as itself, and the skin of its stomach can stretch to accommodate its victim. It has no red pigment in the blood and consequently appears to be almost transparent. **5.** The Sabre Toothed Dragon fish or Viper Fish feeds on deep sea fish which are enticed within striking distance by a luminous lure above its mouth. **6.** The Moray eel attacks its prey in a snake like manner, rearing up and striking with its open mouth with long, sharp fangs. **7.** The Octopus ranges from 2 feet to 32feet across the tentacles and uses these powerful weapons to seize its prey and then draw it into its beaklike mouth. **8.** The Portuguese Man-o-War is a kind of jellyfish with long tentacles.

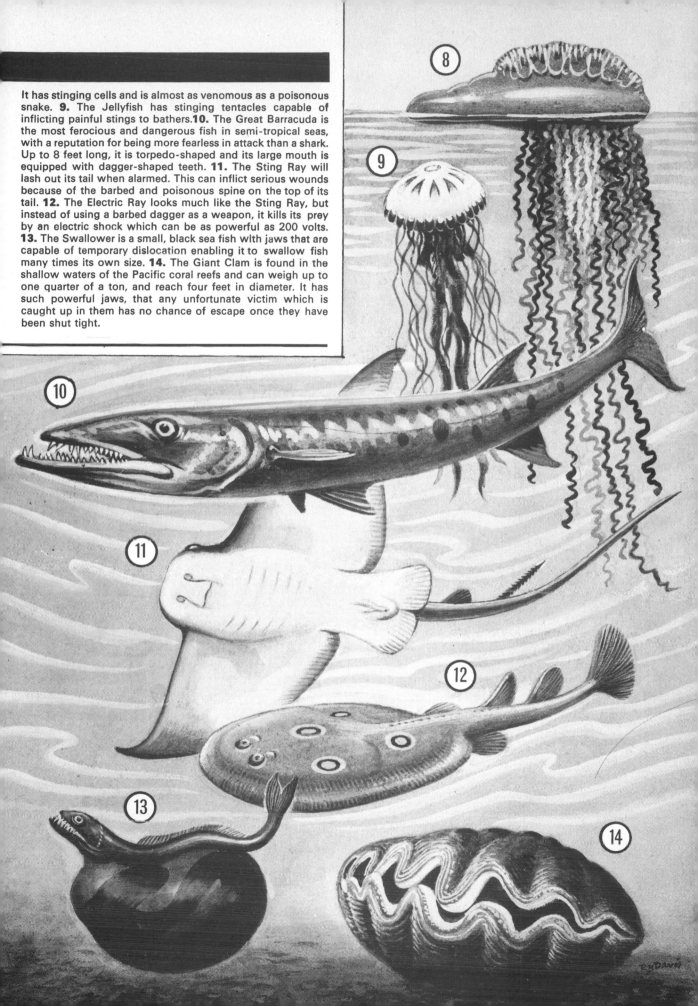

It has stinging cells and is almost as venomous as a poisonous snake. **9.** The Jellyfish has stinging tentacles capable of inflicting painful stings to bathers. **10.** The Great Barracuda is the most ferocious and dangerous fish in semi-tropical seas, with a reputation for being more fearless in attack than a shark. Up to 8 feet long, it is torpedo-shaped and its large mouth is equipped with dagger-shaped teeth. **11.** The Sting Ray will lash out its tail when alarmed. This can inflict serious wounds because of the barbed and poisonous spine on the top of its tail. **12.** The Electric Ray looks much like the Sting Ray, but instead of using a barbed dagger as a weapon, it kills its prey by an electric shock which can be as powerful as 200 volts. **13.** The Swallower is a small, black sea fish with jaws that are capable of temporary dislocation enabling it to swallow fish many times its own size. **14.** The Giant Clam is found in the shallow waters of the Pacific coral reefs and can weigh up to one quarter of a ton, and reach four feet in diameter. It has such powerful jaws, that any unfortunate victim which is caught up in them has no chance of escape once they have been shut tight.

Dick Hellyer found his father fitting the telescopic sight to his .300 rifle. It was not often that Mr Hellyer took the rifle from the locked gun cabinet, and Dick must have shown his interest and surprise.

"The Forestry people rang up," said his father." They've got a killer Roe buck in the Okehurst Plantations, and they want me to scupper him. Like to come? It'll mean an early start in the morning."

"Yes, I would," said Dick emphatically.

"What on earth is a *killer* Roe buck? They don't kill each other. They're harmless, except for nibbling young trees, and a few turnips and things."

"And our rose bushes last summer," laughed his father. Dick laughed too.

"But they don't kill," he said.

"This one can," said Mr Hellyer, but he's a very rare chap. I've never heard of one in Sussex before."

His work completed he put the rifle aside and explained to his twelve year old son about killer deer. Dick learned that very occasionally a buck was born, which when it grew up, had abnormal antlers. Instead of having antlers with the points or tines spreading from them, the abnormal-headed deer grew a pair of sharp dagger-like horns. Every time he shed them in the normal fashion, they were replaced in the Spring by longer and stronger spikes. Dick looked puzzled. "Why does that make him a killer?" he asked.

"Normally," said his father, a buck's antlers are more a form of protection than weapons of attack. When they are fighting in the mating season, their battles are trials of strength. Their antlers interlock and the bucks wrestle and push. The strongest one wins. Its yerv rare for any damage to be done,

but the long straight bayonets on a killer's head don't interlock, they go straight through the other buck's defences. In the Autumn, when they fight, the buck's antlers are at their strongest. A Forester found one dead a few days ago, stabbed right through the ribs. One wound through the heart, and another six inches further back."

Father and son crouched at the edge of the larch plantation. They had been there, still and silent since dawn two hours before.

"We'll give him half an hour," Mr Hellyer whispered. "This is where he's been seen, out in the field." Dick nodded, and then from behind them came a sharp coughing bark.

THE KILLER BUCK'S CHALLENGE

A killer Roe buck was roaming the countryside, and he would have to be caught before any more deer were stabbed to death by its long, lethal antlers . . . .

"Roe Buck," mouthed Mr Hellyer silently. From another plantation at the far side of the field, three hundred yards away came an answering challenge. There was a crashing in the undergrowth, and a gleaming red-brown buck arched over the rabbit wire fence at the edge of the wood. The roe galloped into the field and stopped, head raised. Carefully Mr Hellyer stood up, slipping forward the safety catch on the rifle. This was the killer. Nine inches long, his dagger antlers pointed towards his distant challenger. He barked once. Dick could see the bright body shake as the little deer expelled his breath. His father squeezed the trigger. The crossed hair lines of the telescopic sight rested on the bucks shoulder. The beautiful creature bounded into the air, and galloped straight towards his hidden adversary. Mr Hellyer lowered his rifle.

"Couldn't take the chance of a running shot," he said. "We'll try again this evening."

When they reached their hiding place at the edge of the field, thunder was muttering in the distance, and to the south a flicker of lightning ran along the dark ridge of the Downs. Two does picked their dainty way across the field, followed by a magnificent buck, and again from somewhere in the larch plantation came the short, sharp coughing bark.

"He's there," murmured Mr Hellyer, smiling. Twilight had come, and suddenly the world was lit by a white-blue flash of lightening. Three seconds later the thunder crashed in a tearing, ripping cresendo of bellowing sound, and the echoes rolled away into the distance.

The killer was soon racing across the field towards the buck and the two does, who stood beneath the spreading branches of a great lone oak tree. On his approach, the does retreated demurely, and the two bucks faced each other, heads lowered, breathing defiance. The lightning came down, a blue-white flash. The thunder seemed to shake the ground with its apaalling retching snarl. For a second the oak tree blossomed with a scarlet flower of flame, riven to its base. Smoke rose tenuously from the stricken tree, as the big buck and the does galloped for the woods. The killer lay still, his fierce heart still for ever.

The wind came, and then the first cold drops of rain. Father and son ran for the shelter of the car.

"It wasn't his fault that he was a killer," said Dick. "I'm glad you didn't have to shoot him, Dad."

"So am I," said his father.

WILDLIFE CRISIS

Two kinds of rhinoceros are now in extreme danger. Both the Great Indian rhino and the Sumatran rhino are extremely rare and every effort has now to be made in order to protect them (below).

The Giant Panda is the symbol of an international organization pledged to save the fast disappearing wildlife of the world.

High powered rifles, poisoned arrows, wire snares and batteries of machine guns are the deadly weapons with which poachers prey upon the valuable elephants of Kenya.

Whether they are local tribesmen, hunters on safari, or tough, professional gangs who shoot at herds of animals by the dozen, the result is always the same—another number to add to the alarming death toll of the elephant population in Kenya.

For elephants, as everyone knows, possess ivory tusks, and ivory is highly prized.

Since the middle of 1973 the value of ivory has increased enormously, and because of this, more and more poachers are hunting down elephants to gain money for their tusks of ivory. The tusks are first sold to a dealer and pass through a series of other dealers, before being smuggled out of Mombassa to the Far East where the demand by ivory craftsmen is never ending.

It was in September of 1973 that war was finally declared on these ruthless poachers and dealers by the Kenya National Park Field Forces and the Kenya Police Airwing. An immediate ban was placed on all elephant hunting and ivory dealing.

The elephant of Kenya is, unfortunately, only one of the animals threatened by Man.

Year by year it is becoming more and more important to protect the thousands of different wild animals in the world which

The dedicated men whose lives are devoted to the protection and preservation of wild animals, often risk life and limb to save the creatures in their territory. To capture and transport a rhinoceros from one part of a game reserve to another calls for both skill and courage.

Elephants (above) both in Asia and Africa have been ruthlessly hunted for their valuable ivory tusks. Today, poachers are caught by means of aircraft and helicopters (below.)

are faced with extinction.

Over the centuries, man has torn down forests and jungles, used up fertile valleys for hydro-electric power, dug deep into the earth for valuable minerals, in his desire for 'progress' and to make a better world in which to live.

He has taken over vast tracts of land for the purpose of building towns and cities, giant factory complexes, and highly mechanised farming systems.

And every time he uses up a piece of land, he disrupts the whole, intricate order and system of relationships of living things. The natural habitat of hundreds of wild animals and plants is soon destroyed and the animals themselves begin to disappear.

The last dodo died three hundred years ago as a result of man's work, the great auk became extinct in 1844 and it was over 75 years ago, that the last of the world's beautiful passenger pigeons died.

Sometimes, man has managed to realise before it is too late that certain animals in danger of extinction, should be saved. In the Galapagos Islands years of ruthless killing of a giant tortoise made the creature very rare. Man was at last forbidden to kill the reptile and as a result it was saved and still exists today.

One organisation, established in 1961, is determined to save the world's wildlife before it is too late. This is the World Wildlife Fund which has, over the past decade or so, launched world-wide campaigns in a desperate effort to make people understand, the need for saving wildlife now at all costs.

For, by the year 2,000, it is very possible that no wild animals will exist at all.

Today there are 817 species threatened with extinction, and unless we want to see a world without wildlife in twenty-five years' time, we must all do something to actively involve ourselves in the fight to keep the wild animals of the world alive. And the time to do that is now, before we find, as many of our ancestors did, that we are too late.

These beautiful zebras are becoming more and more rare and, like so many animals in the world today, must be carefully protected to stop them from dying out.

Poachers use all kinds of lethal weapons, including rifles and machine guns, to shoot down elephants.

SILKEN MAGIC

Spiders' webs are very useful things, both to the spiders and to man.

The silk produced by spiders is manufactured in certain glands in its body. It is then forced through many tiny holes in the spider's spinnerets, which are the organs on the underside of the body. As soon as the liquid reaches the air it becomes sticky and strong. No other creatures use silk in so many different ways as the spider. They make it into houses, diving bells, cocoons and traps. One kind of spider even makes a web under water and fills it with air.

At Chester Cathedral there is a painting of the Madonna and Child which is painted on a spider's web and framed between two sheets of glass (below). The picture on the left shows police searching for a criminal who was hiding behind a locked door. They felt he could not be there because a spider's web covered the knob and keyhole.

Until recently, the hairlines in a theodolite (above) were made with split strands of spider's silk. This is an instrument for measuring angles used by surveyors for making plans and maps.

One kind of spider uses its thread as a form of parachute (above right). Carried upwards by the air currents, it may travel for many miles. Equally fascinating is the early belief that cobwebs had medicinal qualities. They were used to stop the flow of blood from a wound (right), perhaps because they aided the blood's congealing characteristics.

NATURE QUIZ

Now that you have read the nature section of this book, see how many of the questions you can answer in the quiz below. The answers are at the back of the book.

1. A wood consists of several levels or layers. What is the name of the lowest level?

2. In which layer does the tawny owl roost?

3. Certain substances in the soil called 'decomposers' such as fungi and bacteria have a very important job to do. What is their job?

4. Name the two deer which are native to Britain.

5. From which country does the Sika come?

6. Who is believed to have brought Fallow Deer to Britain?

7. Gilbert White became famous for the book he published on the observations he made about the natural history of his village. What was the book called?

8. Who is often called the father of English natural history?

9. In 1802 George Montagu published his famous book. What was it called?

10. What was the name of the ship on which Darwin sailed as expedition naturalist?

11. What was the title of Darwin's famous book in which he put forward his theory of evolution?

12. Bushbabies are long-legged acrobats of which family?

13. Which animal, found in America, does the African Zorilla closely resemble?

14. What is the favourite food of the Aardvark?

15. The 'Scorpion' fish is striped like a zebra and has powerful, poisonous spines. What is this creature's other name?

16. What is a Portuguese Man-O-War?

17. Why is the Swallower so-called?

18. When was the World Wildlife Fund set up?

19. Which sea bird became extinct in 1844.

20. What exactly are the spinnerets of a spider?

The Arts

Diplomat With A Paintbrush

If Rubens had never held a paintbrush, had never painted even one picture, we would probably still know of his name today. For, as well as being the painter who dominated the golden age of Flemish art, Rubens was also an eminently successful diplomat.

The brilliant young artist, fresh from his home in Antwerp, arrived in Italy to enter the service of the wealthy Duke of Mantua. The year was 1600, and at the astonishingly early age of twenty-three Pater Paul Rubens, court painter, had begun what was to be one of the most amazingly brilliant and successful careers in the history of art.

Yet to everyone who knew his family, the idea of a remarkable future ahead for the young boy was inconceivable. For the circumstances of Rubens' childhood had little to recommend themselves to the achievement of wealth and fame.

When Rubens was born on June 28th, 1577, his father was serving a detention sentence at Siegen in Westphalia. A lawyer and alderman at Antwerp of Protestant sympathies, Jan Rubens was suspected as a Calvinist and escaped with his wife to Cologne in 1568. An offence against William of Orange led to his imprisonment and then to house arrest in Siegen.

When Rubens was ten years old his father died and his kind, good-hearted mother took her son back to Antwerp where he completed his education.

Rubens soon decided what he wanted to do in life. His mother did not discourage his ambition to be a painter, and sent him to be a student under three Antwerp masters. Rubens learnt first from the landscape painter Tobias van Helcht, then from Adam van Noort, the religious painter and finally most important of all, from Otto van Veen, court painter to the Regents of the Southern Netherlands, Archduke Albert and his wife the Infanta Isabella.

It was van Veen who introduced the young Rubens to art patrons and through these he was recommended to Vincenzo Gonzago, the Duke of Mantua, who decided to appoint the artist as his court painter.

Rubens stayed in Italy for eight years and travelled to all the important art cities, studying classical sculpture, copying the Italian Renaissance masters for the Duke of Mantua and for his own instruction, and was also able to observe an important event

105

St. George and the Dragon by Rubens

which was taking place in the art of Italy at th
time: the movement from mannerism to baroqu
It was to be in the style of baroque art that Ruber
would excel. His studies in Italy gave him a dee
knowledge of the three giants of the High Renais
ance, Michelangelo, Leonardo and Raphael, an
these soon became his idols.

Then in 1608, he was called back to Antwerp
the news of his mother's illness. But to his great ar
lasting sorrow, Rubens did not get home in time t
see his mother alive.

Rubens had been away for eight years, and whe
he returned he was a mature, experienced and high
gifted painter. Commissions for pictures began t
pour in almost immediately. From home and abroa
the requests for his work flooded in and pupi
began to flock to his studio to learn from the 'master
Over the next ten years Rubens completed a grea
number of works including two masterpieces i
Antwerp Cathedral, *The Rising of the Cross* and *Th
Descent of the Cross*. The year 1617 saw the com
pletion of a wonderful figure painting *The Miraculou
Draught of Fish*.

In 1610 he married the beautiful Isabella Bran
and built a fine house in Antwerp which became th
pride of the city. It was a model of the Pantheon an
Rubens took great delight in filling it with classica
sculptures and other precious antiques.

Early in 1622 Rubens was summonned to th
court of Marie de Medici in Paris and was commiss
ioned to produce twenty-one huge paintings for th
great gallery in the Luxembourg Palace. From tha
time on, the fame of his European studio knew n
bounds and commissions came in in ever-increasing
numbers.

But if Rubens had never touched a paintbrush
had never painted even one picture, we woulc
probably still know of his name today. His handsome
courtly appearance, his intellectual gifts and pro-
ficiency as a linguist all combined to make hirr
eminently suited for the high-ranking diplomatic
role he was called upon to play by the Infanta Isabella
His work as a diplomat took him on journeys to
Paris, London, Madrid and Amsterdam, and everywhere he went he was asked to produce paintings.
Rubens plunged into his diplomatic career with a
deep belief in the possibilities of peace between the
Netherlands and Spain, and between the Kings of
Spain and England. His negotiations for peace were
a great success and, having laid down the founda-
tions for a peace treaty between England and Spain,
he was rewarded for his work both as a diplomat and
as an artist by King Charles I with a knighthood.
From 1830 until his death ten years later, Rubens

San Pedro by Rubens

gave all his time to the work he loved most and after leaving England went back to his giant studio in Antwerp to carry out the thousands of commissions he had received. The studio, 45 feet by 35 feet in size and the additional workshops above it, formed a giant 'factory of art' where Rubens was assisted in his work by such great artists as Van Dyck, and Jan Brueghel.

Rubens' first wife had died in 1626 and in 1630 he married again. A year later he bought a country mansion where the beauty of the scenery inspired him to produce the great Flemish landscapes of his later years.

One of the most prolific and wide ranging of all artists, Rubens never ceases to amaze art historians by the brilliance and power he achieved in so many different kinds of painting.

On May 30th 1640, the artist who had dominated the golden age of Flemish art, died at the age of sixty-three.

Today, more than three hundred years after his death, Rubens remains unchallenged as the most prodigious and productive of all the great European artists.

Rubens studied under three Antwerp masters (above). His work as a high-ranking diplomat took him to London, and King Charles I was so pleased with the peace treaty he had arranged between England and Spain, that he rewarded the artist with a knighthood. (below).

A MAN AMONGST MEN

Torrential currents and menacing rocks could tear apart home-made boats in seconds.

It was one of the most treacherous death traps in America's frozen North, but there were thousands of men willing to risk their lives to pass through it in the year of 1898. For the men who set out on the long, tough, trail to the Klondike that year were determined to strike gold at any price, and for the chance to do that they had first to travel through the terrifying Miles Canyon.

But there were many who did not even live to get that far. To reach the Canyon, they had first to cross over the fatally perilous White and Chilkoot Passes and even those who did manage to get through the Canyon, had then to face the dreaded White Horse Rapids where torrential currents and menacing rocks could tear apart their home-made boats in seconds.

There were, however, many tough travellers who did complete the Klondike trail and start their search for gold, and one of them was a young adventurer from San Francisco called Jack London.

He had set out to make his fortune and a year later, he returned home, sick with scurvy and with only a handful of gold dust worth four and a half dollars. But Jack London *did* make his fortune—through *not* finding gold in the Klondike Rush of '98. For the rest of his life he was to write hundreds of stories about his experiences and the people he had come across in America's far North West on his journeys of danger and adventure. For there were millions of people who paid to read those stories and, from the sale of his books, Jack London became a rich man.

He was born in the heart of America's most spectacular frontier, San Francisco where the rush to the Klondike began. London has told his own account of his early life, and from this we can see how determined he was to make a better life for himself:

"My father was Pennsylvania-born, a soldier, a scout, backwoodsman, trapper and wanderer. My mother was born in Ohio. Both came west independently, meeting and marrying in San Francisco where I was born January 12, 1876. What little city life I then passed was in my babyhood. My life, from my fourth to nine years, was spent upon Californian ranches. I learned to read and write about my fifth year, though I do not remember anything about it. I could always read and write . . . . Folks say that I simply insisted on being taught. Was an omniverous reader, principally because reading matter was scarce and I had to be grateful for whatsoever fell into my hands."

At 15, Jack was the family breadwinner, having to work twelve hours a day in a canning factory for a pittance that barely kept his mother and two step sisters in food and clothes. But there were two activities which brightened up the boy's life; reading and rowing boats. It was not long before he decided to escape from the slave labour of the factory. "At fifteen," he wrote proudly, "I was a man amongst men . . . the adventure lust was strong in me and I left home." With three hundred dollars which he borrowed from friends, London bought his own sloop, the *Razzle Dazzle* and during the twelve adventurous months of 1892 he raided the oyster beds in his boat and earned the nickname "Prince of the Oyster Pirates." He worked at other jobs too, spent three days in jail, and went on a political rally.

Jack's career as an oyster pirate ended when he fell into the bay and almost drowned. He had been able to make more money in a night than he had in a month at the dreaded factory and, knowing that his crimes warranted up to 500 years in prison, he decided to go away to sea and stop the life of crime he had been living.

In 1893 London became an able-bodied seaman on the *Sophia Sutherland* and spent three months hunting seals in the seas around the world.

In January 1893 he signed up as an able bodied seaman on the *Sophia Sutherland* and spent three months hunting seals in the seas around the world.

After trying his hand at numerous, poorly paid jobs, Jack decided to go back to school. He was 19, four years older than everyone else in his class, and three years later he entered the University of California. He never finished the course. For on July 25th, 1897 Jack joined the gold-seeking stampede to the North.

"It was in the Klondike I found myself," he later wrote,". There no-body talks. Everybody thinks. You get your perspective. I got mine."

After returning from his adventure--packed trip to the Klondike, London began to write stories about his life, and found many magazines that were prepared to pay him well for his work. In 1902 he went to London to investigate the terrible conditions of the East End and for six weeks, he lived among the sick, half-starved men and women who gave the title of the book, *The People of the Abyss*. He wandered about the streets in dirty ragged clothes, and slept and ate in a workhouse.Five years after his return from the Klondike, the book which was to make Jack London famous throughout the world was published. *The Call of the Wild*, with its story about Buck, the dog who was taken to Alaska to work as a sledge puller for the Klondike gold miners, has captured the imaginations of people all over the globe since its publication in 1903. From that time on, London never suffered poverty again. More best-selling novels poured from his pen, *The Sea Wolf*, *The Game*, *Cruise of the Dazzler*, *White Fang*, and *Cruise of the Snark*.

In 1904 London became a reporter on the Russo-Japanese War and

The American writer spent six months in London, wandered about the East End dressed in dirty, ragged clothes.

two years later wrote a stirring account of the earthquake of 1906 which devasted his birthplace, San Francisco.

Then, he went on a world cruise in an attempt to sail round the world and after 27 months at sea was forced to return home after being struck down with a tropical illness.

After one more adventurous voyage, he settled down on his ranch at California, and in 1916 took his own life. The wild, impetuous adventurer who had become the most popular and highest paid writer in America was dead.

An extract from London's own brilliantly written account of his trip to the North-West, from 'Through the Rapids to the Klondike', describing the journey throughthe treacherous Miles Canyon, referred to as 'the Box' by the writer.

Lashing the steering oar so that it could not possibly escape, I allotted my comrades their places; for I was captain. Merrit Sloper, direct from adventures in South America and who knew a little of boating, took his position in the bow with a paddle. Thompson and Goodman, landlubbers who had never rowed before this trip, were stationed side by side at the oars . . .

"Be sure to keep on the ridge," cried the men on the bank as we cast off.

The water, though swift, had a slick, oily appearance until we dashed into the very jaws of the Box, where it instantly took on the aspect of chaos broken loose. Afraid that the rowers might catch a crab or make some other disastrous fumble I called the oars in.

Then we met it on the fly. I caught a glimpse of the spectators fringing the brink of the cliffs above, and another glimpse of the rock walls dashing by like twin lightning express trains; then my whole energy was concentrated in keeping to the ridge. This was serrated with stiff waves which the boat, dead with weight, could not mount, being forced to jab her nose through at every lunge. For all the peril, I caught myself smiling at the ridiculous capers cut by Sloper, perched on the very bow and working his paddle like mad. Just as he would let drive for a tremendous strike, the stern would fall in a trough, jerking the bow clear up, and he would miss the water utterly. And at the next stroke perhaps, the nose would dive clean under almost sweeping him away—and he only weighed one hundred pounds. But never did he lose his presence of mind or grit. Once, he turned and cried some warning at the top of his lungs, but it was drowned in the pandemonium of sound. The next instant we fell off the Ridge. The water came aboard in all directions, and the boat, caught in a transverse current, threatened to twin broadside. This would mean destruction. I threw myself against the sweep till I could hear it cracking, while Sloper snapped his paddle short off.

And all this time we were flying down the gutter, less than two yards from the wall. Several times it seemed all up with us; but finally, mounting the Ridge almost sidewise, we took a header through a tremendous comber and shot into the whirlwind pool of the great circular court.

Ordering out the oars for steerage-way, and keeping a close eye on the split currents, I caught one free breath before we flew into the second half of the canyon. Though we crossed the Ridge from left to right and back again, it was merely a repetition of the first half. A moment later the *Yukon Belle* rubbed softly against the wall. We had run the mile of the canyon in two minutes by the watch.

Children's Illustrators...

*One of the most popular illustrators of the last two centuries was Arthur Rackham (1867-1939). His most characteristic and best known illustrations are for children's books, particularly for fairy stories. His first real success was with **Grimm's Fairy Tales** in 1900. In 1905 he produced **Rip Van Winkle** and in 1939 the year of his death, his most famous work, **Wind In The Willows**, written by the brilliant Scottish author, Kenneth Grahame.*

When Lilies of the day are done,
And sunk the golden westering sun.

Walter Crane, who lived from 1845 to 1915, was one of the most successful and prolific illustrators of children's books at the end of the nineteenth century. In all his books, *Crane reveals great imagination and skill in being able to combine words and pictures in beautiful harmony, as you can see from the illustration from Flora's Feast above.*

...The Artists Who Help To Bring Stories To Life

Many of the characters and stories we read about in books when we are young remain in our minds for years and years. This is usually because the books are well written by authors who have the special gift of story telling with words that make their characters come alive from the page as we read. Very often a writer is helped to tell his story by means of illustrations which can make our reading of the book even more entertaining and satisfying.

The art of the book illustrator is a very skilled and specialised one, requiring a deep understanding of the mood and atmosphere of a story, and the very rare gift of portraying characters in a way which the author had imagined them to look in his mind.

Sometimes, with really talented artists, the illustrations they create for books are able to stand on their own as individual works of art. As you can see from the work of the children's book illustrators shown in this feature, the illustrations of books can be as important as the words themselves.

SIR JOHN TENNIEL

The artist who became world-famous as the illustrator of Lewis Carroll's *Alice* books was born on February 28th, 1820. After leaving the Royal Academy, Tenniel sent his first picture to the exhibition of the Society of British Arts at the age of sixteen. Nine years later he was commissioned to paint a fresco for the Upper Waiting Hall in the House of Lords, and in 1850 was invited to fill the position of joint cartoonist, with John Leech on *Punch* magazine.

The work he did for this publication included about 2,300 cartoons, hundreds of minor drawings, double page cartoons for *Punch's Almanac*, and 250 designs for *Punch's Pocket Books*. It was for his work as an artist and humourist that Tenniel was knighted in 1893.

But it was by his illustrations for books that Tenniel achieved international fame, and his drawings for *Alice's Adventures In Wonderland* 1866, and *Through The Looking Glass* 1870, has made the name of Sir John Tenniel immortal.

RALPH STEADMAN

Many artists, apart from Tenniel, have illustrated Lewis Carroll's *Alice*, the latest of whom is Ralph Steadman. His picture of Humpty-Dumpty can be seen on the right.

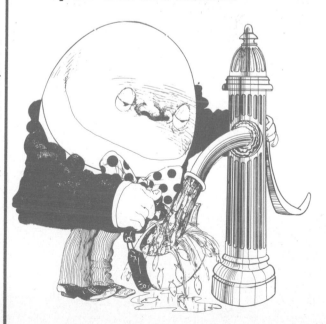

'PHIZ'

Not many people have heard the name Halbot Knight Browne, but millions know this English artist by his pseudonym, 'Phiz'. Famous throughout the world as one of the most successful and brilliant interpreters and illustrators of the novels of Dickens, Browne adopted this rather peculiar name so that it would harmonise with Dickens' own pseudonym of 'Boz'.

Browne was born at Lambeth in London on June 15th, 1815, the son of poor and humble parents. As a boy he was apprenticed to the engraver William Finden where he received his only artistic education. When he was 19 years old, Browne left engraving to pursue other artistic work and two years later met Charles Dickens who was looking for a talented illustrator for his serial stories. Browne submitted his drawings to the novelist and was given the job.

It was the work he did for Dickens, especially in *Pickwick Papers*, *Dombey and Son*, *David Copperfield*, *Bleak House* and *Martin Chuzzlewit*, that established Brown's reputation as a book illustrator. His work was much in demand and he received commissions from many publishers, including the illustrations for the best known novels of Charles Lever and Harrison Ainsworth. Then, in 1867, Browne was srtuck with paralysis and was unable to draw again. He never achieved his boyhood ambition to become famous as a painter, but he had become very popular and highly respected as an illustrator. And today, his works are reprinted over and over again in new editions of the novels by one of the world's most famous and popular of writers, Charles Dickens.

GEORGE CRUIKSHANK

*P*erhaps the most famous book illustration in the world is George Cruikshank's drawing, Asking For More in Oliver Twist, the novel by Charles Dickens. Cruikshank, who was born in London on September 27th, 1792, was to become one of England's most successful caricaturists and illustrators. While still in his teens, he had already become a poular artist, without the benefit of any formal art training.

As a boy he could turn his hand to all kinds of art forms. He helped his father, who was a painter, to produce etchings and designs and before he reached twenty had achieved popular recognition as a highly talented artist. Cruikshank was a born humourist and he produced hundreds of satirical cartoons and drawings for magazines.

Far a generation, Cruikshank satirised all the political parties of his time. He poked fun at Tories, Whigs and Radicals with refreshing impartiality, and he found something humourous to say about every public event which took place in his day.

Whatever his subject, whether it was wars, the enemies of England, the court, the Church, low life and high life, Cruikshank showed the caricaturist's spirited sense of humour, and the artist's technical skill.

Cruickshank died on February 1st, 1878, at the age of 86 and was buried in St. Pauls Cathedral.

Among his most famous book illustrations are The Humourist, Life in London, *Grimm's* Collection of German Popular Stories, *for which he created twenty two wonderful etchings,* Jack Shephard, Guy Fawkes, The Ingoldsby Legends *and, of course, the unforgettable,* Oliver Twist.

the Royal Institute of Painters in Water Colours. In the years 1891, 1894, and 1898 she exhibited many water colours and illustrations from her books at the Fine Art society.

From 1883 to 1897 she issued a series of Kate Greenaway Almanacs. She nearly always wrote the text for the books she illustrated, although she did create illustrations for Pied Piper Of Hamelin.

She died in Hampstead, London, on November 6th, 1901.

EDWARD ARDIZZONE

Edward Ardizzone is among the most famous of the contemporary illustrators of children's books. He began to write and illustrate his delightful series of Tim books in 1936, and became famous as a brilliant war artist during the Second World War. In 1941 he published Baggage To The Enemy, a book about his experiences as a war artist, and six years later produced illustrations for Bunyan's Pilgrim's Progress. The picture above is from Ardizzone's book, Nicholas And The Fast-Moving Diesel.

KATE GREENAWAY

*O*riginality and charm are the hallmarks of Kate Greenaway's beautiful illustrations.

She was born in London on March 17th, 1846 and at the age of twenty-two began to exhibit some of her drawings and had her first illustrations published in varoius magazines, including one called Little Folks.

In 1879 she produced her first successful book, Under The Window and this was followed by The Birthday Book, Mother Goose, Little Ann and other books for children. All these were tremendously popular and became highly valued by art experts. These little works, usually called 'Toy-books', created a revolution in book illustration. Leading art critics throughout the world praised the brilliant work of Kate Greenaway, including John Ruskin, Ernest Chesneau and Arsene Alexandre in France, and Richard Muther in Germany.

In 1890 Miss Greenaway was elected a member of

BEATRIX POTTER

The books of Beatrix Potter have been loved by countless numbers of children all over the world. Her delightful animal characters of Peter Rabbit, Benjamin Bunny, Jemima Puddle-Duck, Mrs Tiggy-Winkle and many more have made children laugh with delight, sob with sadness, or simply, kept them absorbed with rapturous interest for hours at a time. Beatrix Potter developed her love of nature from a very early age. She was born in London on July 6th, 1866, and spent a very lonely, repressed childhood as the only daughter of extremely strict, conventional parents. Only on her annual holidays to Scotland or to the Lake District, did Beatrix find fun and adventure in her otherwise restricted life. These holidays gave her her first experience of the country and helped her to develop her wonderful talent for drawing animals and plants; drawings which she later used in imaginative watercolours.

When she was 27 years old and still living at home, Beatric began to write the first of her picture letters. The eldest child of her former companion and German teacher became ill in September, 1893, and to cheer him up, Beatrix decided to send him an illustrated letter. In it she told him about Peter Rabbit. This letter was followed by many others, and the delight and pleasure which they gave to the sick child, encouraged Beatrix to write about the adventures of Peter Rabbit for a book. She had made up stories about many other characters and wrote about them in letters sent to her teachers other children. Then, in 1902 The Tale of Peter Rabbit was published privately. Eventually, she found a publisher, Frederick Warne & Co., who brought out twenty-three of her little books for children. They have been published in many languages and have made the name of Beatrix Potter famous throughout the world.

ERNEST H. SHEPHARD

Everyone who has read Kenneth Grahame's *Wind In The Willows* or A. A. Milne's *Winnie the Pooh* and Christopher Robin books, will remember the delightful drawings used to illustrate the stories.

The artists who drew them was Ernest H. Shepard, and it is from his illustrations that we know how Winnie the Pooh, Piglet, Rat, Mole, Toad and Christopher Robin actually *looked* like.

Indeed, it is very difficult to think of these characters without seeing them through Shepard's eyes because he helped so much to bring them alive to the reader.

Ernest Shapard was born in St. John's Wood in London in 1879. When only seven years old, he drew three remarkable portraits of his aunts, showing the first hints of the wonderful talent for drawing which he was to develop, at a very early age.

In 1901 he exhibited his work for the first time at the Royal Academy, and during the first fifty years or so of this century, he was a regular contributor to the famous *Punch* magazine, as Cruikshank and Tenniel were before him.

But it is for his charming pictures of characters in children's books that Ernest Shepard is famous, and it is these which have delighted hundreds of thousands of children for so many years.

He has written and illustrated an account of his own early childhood in *Drawn From Memory*, in which he describes his life with his family in London, in the country and at the seaside. He has written as well as illustrated two other books, *Ben and Brock* and *Betsy and Joe*. And in these and other books, the charm and humour of Ernest Shepards' work live in the memory long after they have been read.

RODIN the Revolutionary

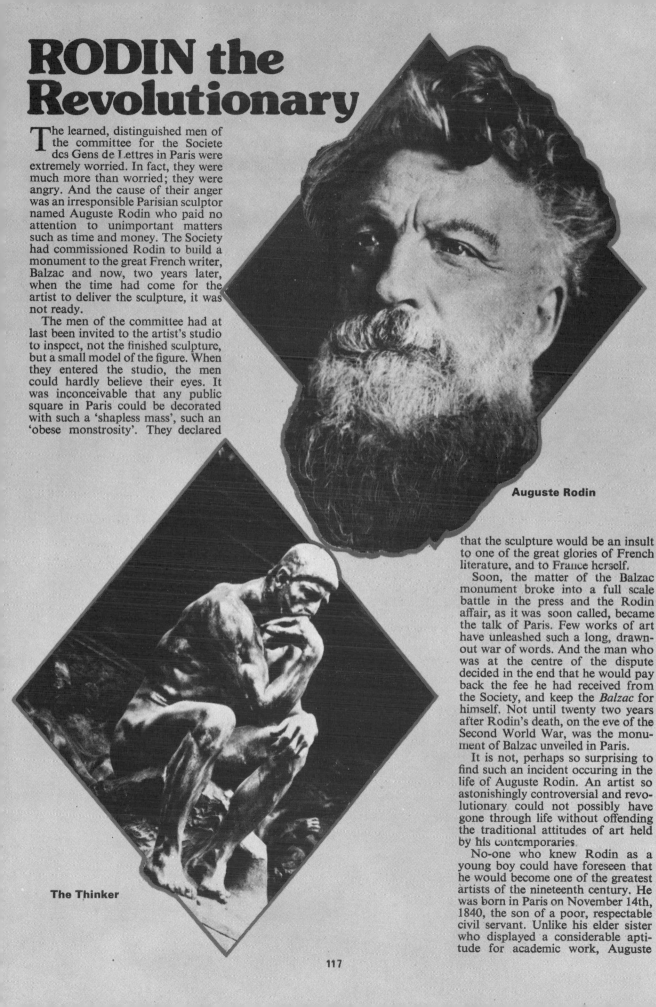

The learned, distinguished men of the committee for the Societe des Gens de Lettres in Paris were extremely worried. In fact, they were much more than worried; they were angry. And the cause of their anger was an irresponsible Parisian sculptor named Auguste Rodin who paid no attention to unimportant matters such as time and money. The Society had commissioned Rodin to build a monument to the great French writer, Balzac and now, two years later, when the time had come for the artist to deliver the sculpture, it was not ready.

The men of the committee had at last been invited to the artist's studio to inspect, not the finished sculpture, but a small model of the figure. When they entered the studio, the men could hardly believe their eyes. It was inconceivable that any public square in Paris could be decorated with such a 'shapeless mass', such an 'obese monstrosity'. They declared

Auguste Rodin

The Thinker

that the sculpture would be an insult to one of the great glories of French literature, and to France herself.

Soon, the matter of the Balzac monument broke into a full scale battle in the press and the Rodin affair, as it was soon called, became the talk of Paris. Few works of art have unleashed such a long, drawn-out war of words. And the man who was at the centre of the dispute decided in the end that he would pay back the fee he had received from the Society, and keep the *Balzac* for himself. Not until twenty two years after Rodin's death, on the eve of the Second World War, was the monument of Balzac unveiled in Paris.

It is not, perhaps so surprising to find such an incident occuring in the life of Auguste Rodin. An artist so astonishingly controversial and revolutionary could not possibly have gone through life without offending the traditional attitudes of art held by his contemporaries.

No-one who knew Rodin as a young boy could have foreseen that he would become one of the greatest artists of the nineteenth century. He was born in Paris on November 14th, 1840, the son of a poor, respectable civil servant. Unlike his elder sister who displayed a considerable aptitude for academic work, Auguste

The Kiss

proved a most unpromising pupil at school. Bullied by his fellow-pupils, he was to remain a silent, solitary and highly sensitive figure throughout his school-life. Hopeless at grammar and spelling, the red-haired, tubby young boy left school at the age of thirteen virtually uneducated. The one thing he wanted to do was to draw, for that was the only thing he was interested in. To his unimaginative, practical father, such an idea was preposterous, almost a crime. But with the influence of his kind, understanding sister, Auguste at last received permission from his father to enter a drawing school.

The young Rodin soon discovered what he wanted to do in life. From the moment his hands touched a piece of clay, he realised that for him, life had no other meaning but sculpture.

After three years, Rodin decided that he must go to a more advanced art school. He wanted desperately to attend the famous Grande Ecole des Beaux Arts. To everyone's surprise, the brilliant young student was rejected by the examiners. It is hard to believe that these men could have failed to detect the great talent shown in Rodin's early works, but it more than likely that the academic examiners felt that the artist's work did not fit in with the required conventions of their attitude to art.

With the doors of the Ecole closed, Rodin was to spend the next twenty years trying to find work all over Paris. Always on the verge of poverty, he never lost hope and was saved from the depths of despair by the unceasing joy he found in his work. He was not an ambitious young man and unlike many artists, did not dream of fame and fortune, and would have laughed if he had known that both were to come his way before his death.

But in the meantime, Rodin worked for decorators and sculptors, producing commercial ornaments and doing any work he could find. In his spare time he taught himself to read and then devoured all the great masters of literature, developing a life-long love of the great French poets.

Then, when Rodin was twenty-two, his life was shattered by the death of his beloved sister, Maria. Choked with grief he stayed within the confines of his family's house and left his work untouched for weeks. He decided to join a religious community as a novice and stayed there for nearly two years before he left to resume his craftsmen's existence and went to work at the studio of a commercial sculptor called Carrier-Belleuse.

In 1875, Rodin managed to get one of his works accepted by the Salon in the Louvre. Then with the small amount of money he had saved, Rodin went on a trip to Italy

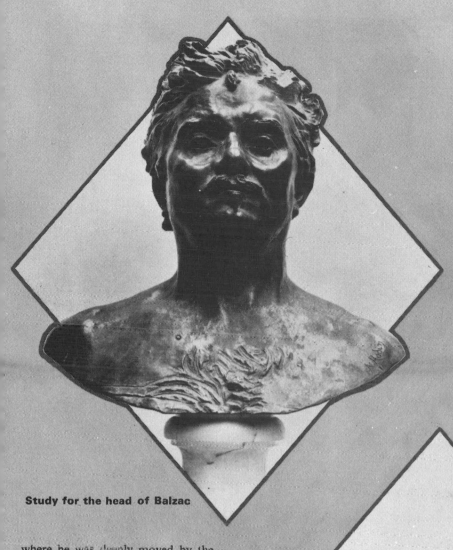

Study for the head of Balzac

By the year 1893, when he was commissioned to produce the Balzac monument, Rodin's ideas had become too free, his imagination too original, for him to accept imposed rules. Balzac had been dead for years when Rodin received the commission. All the artist knew was that Balzac was short, fat and that he worked in his dressing gown. To portray the genius as such and at the same time make him look like the immense, dominating literary figure of his age, was a difficult thing to achieve. But the result was what is believed to be the greatest piece of sculpture of the nineteenth century; some believe the greatest since Michelangelo.

We have seen how Rodin's contemporaries took a very different view of the monument. But by 1900 Rodin's reputation was so high that he received the homage, not only of France, but of all Europe. The man who had defied the artistic traditions and conventions of his age, had, at last, earned the recognition he deserved. Unlike many men of genius, Rodin was able to enjoy the respect and admiration of the world in his own lifetime.

The Burghers of Calais

where he was deeply moved by the works of Michelangelo and Donatello.

After years of disappointment and rejection by the French academics of the art world, Rodin began to get his name known. In 1880 when he exhibited his *John The Baptist Preaching*, and the final figure of the *Bronze Age*, Rodin was able to silence his hostile critics and establish his position in the world of sculpture. The French government decided to commission him to produce a series of bas reliefs for a door at the Museum of Decorative Art. The door was to represent scenes from Dante's *Divine Comedy* and Rodin was to work on this, *The Gate of Hell*, for the rest of his life. For this monumental task, Rodin made over two hundred figures, the most famous of which is *The Thinker*.

In 1884 he began to work on one of his greatest masterpieces, *The Burghers of Calais*, commissioned to be a monument to honour the heroes who offered to sacrifice their lives to save the city from destruction in the 14th century. When shown in 1889 the monument caused a sensation and even Rodin's critics were obliged to congratulate him.

MAKE A MOBILE

One of the most creative and fascinating of modern crafts is the art of mobile making.

A mobile is really a piece of sculpture suspended in the air. As it turns it shows constantly changing designs in form and colour.

It was not until the 1930s that the mobile as a moving sculpture became an art form, and the man who was responsible for this was an American artist, Alexander Calder, the inventor of the mobile.

You can make your mobile as simple, or as complicated as you like. Sometimes, the very simplicity of a shape can be more effective than an intricate design.

Mobiles are usually made out of wire and metal, card, glass, wood, shells.

WHAT YOU WILL NEED:
Scissors, pliers, wire cutters, glue, stapler, needles, threads of various thicknesses and colours, including invisible nylon thread.

MATERIALS TO CHOOSE FROM:
Paper of various thicknesses, card, foil, balsa wood, scraps of string, scraps of fabric, ribbon, felt, beads, sequins, feathers, shells, leaves.

THE SPIRAL—See diagrams 1 and 2.
One of the easiest and most rewarding of designs for mobiles is the spiral. This is made out of paper or card and when hung gives a continuous climbing effect as it turns in a draught of air.

WHAT TO DO:
1. Cut out a circle, 7 inches in diameter from a piece of card or thick paper, in a colour of your choice.
2. Start at point A shown in the diagram and cut continuously until you reach position B. The centre will drop out and you will be left with a spiral.
3. Hang the spiral by means of invisible thread through a tiny hole marked C in the diagram.

Paper is only one of the many materials which can be used in the construction of your mobile. You may wish to design a mobile out of copper wire, using shapes which are purely abstract and not representing animals or birds. For these, it is best to make a sketch of the shape of the mobile and then work from this design.

You may wish to make a mobile out of a twist of copper wire and from this suspend shapes made out of metal. The stringing of this more complicated kind of mobile is vitally important and depends, as all mobiles do, on getting the right balance.

WHAT TO DO:
1. Cut a piece of wire for the lowest bar, about 8 inches long. Bend each end of the wire with pliers, and hang the shapes of metal from nylon thread. The shapes should hang freely below the wire bar.
2. You can make two more, smaller bars and hang more metal shapes from these.

Once you have made a few mobiles like these, you can then start to use your own imagination and design them according to your own ideas, perhaps using other materials we have suggested.

In diagrams 3 and 4 on the opposite page we have shown how to use pressed leaves as hanging decoration from a central construction of metal or card. If metal is used it is cut out in the same way as shown in diagram 1 but care should be taken when doing this and it should not be done without the supervision of an adult.

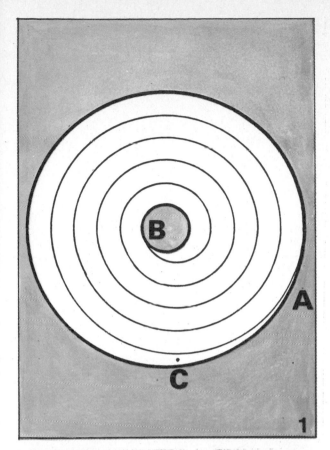

1

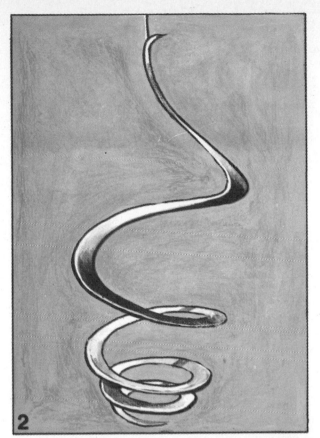

2

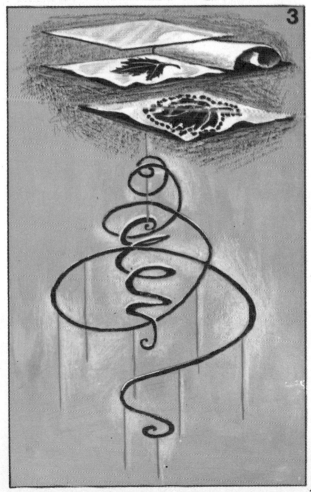

3

4

The Unfinished Monument

The man who spent most of his life at work on the design of the Church of the Holy Family in Barcelona was Gaudi. Since this famous architect's death, the building has remained virtually untouched and still has still to be completed.

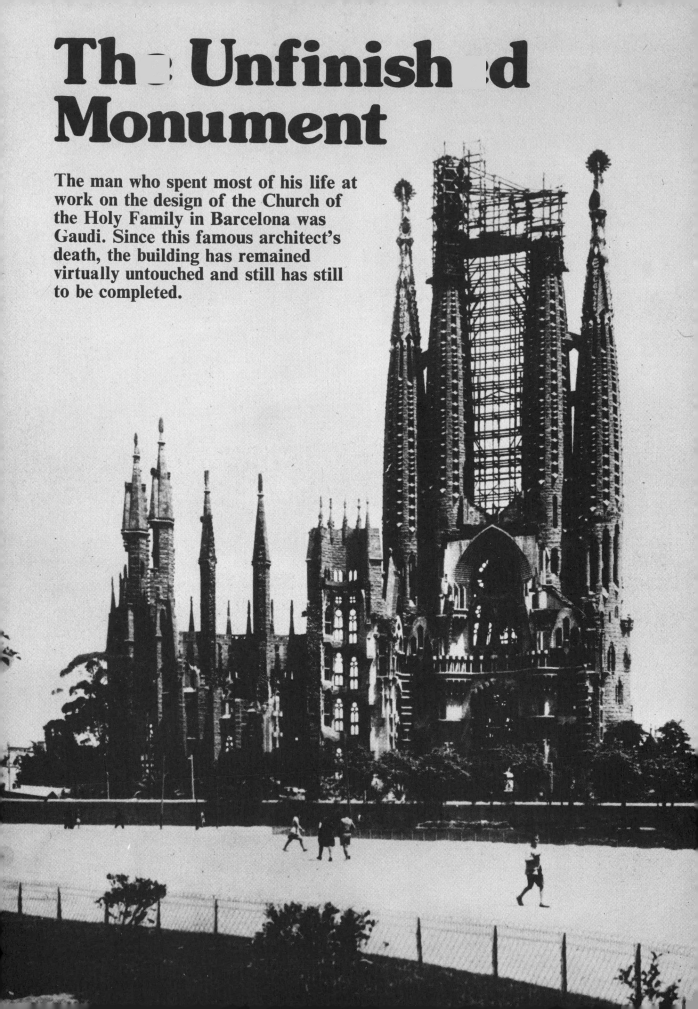

He was the most original architect in Europe during the nineteenth century and certainly the most outstanding figure of architecture in Spain during that period. His name was Antonio Gaudi y Cornet and he was born at Reus in Tarragona on June 26th, 1852.

Gaudi studied at the Barcelona school of architecture and was early recognised as a brilliant architectural inventor and constructor. He built a great number of palaces and houses and restored Medieval monuments such as Palma Cathedral and the Monastery of Monserrat. He combined his own very individual style with a Medieval style in his Bishop's Palace at Astorga which has Gothic towers, battlemets and windows.

The palace and park in Barcelona named after Gaudi's patron, Count Guell shows the originality and inventiveness of the architect's imagination. The Palacio Guell is a six storeyed stone fronted house, while the Parque Guell, now the city's public park, is situated on the outskirts of the town on a hill. It contains a church, a house, arbours, sculpture and playgrounds. Basically a Gothic style, there are Doric columns, and natural motifs such as caves, plants, rocks and animals. The overall impression is one of a fairy-tale garden of magic and fun.

Gaudi found fame and recognition through all these works, but it is for his building of the Church of the Holy Family that he is best remembered. This

Gaudi's highly individual ideas on architecture are illustrated in the design of this house in Barcelona. When this extraordinary architect set out to create a park and palace for his patron Count Guell he produced another masterpiece. The columns shown on the left and the Gatekeeper's Lodge can both be seen in the park situated just outside Barcelona.

massive project was the problem of his life and it remains unfinished to this day.

This church, known as the Templo Expiatorio de la Sagrada Familia, was designed by Francisco del Villar in neo-Gothic style and begun in 1882. In November, 1883 the work was entrusted to his assistant, Gaudi. By 1893 Gaudi had completed the crypt and the outer walls of the chevet, according to Villar's designs but after this Gaudi developed his own ideas on the design of the building. When he had been working at Monserrat Gaudi was fascinated by the formation of the mountain peaks which rise high above Barcelona and he tried to capture this effect, with stunning results, in his construction of the church.

The building was continued after a break during the First World War, in 1919, and work on it was stopped when the architect died on June 7th, 1926.

Since then, the church has remained almost as it was when Gaudi left it. In recent years, work has started again, and we can only hope that one day this wonderful monument will be finished, for it is the greatest ecclesiastical building since the eighteenth century.

The building finished so far, is but a portion of the entire structure. Still to be built are the nave and other transcept, some towers, and the choir cimborio whose tower is designed to rise to about 560 feet, higher than the tallest Medieval church in Europe.

Towering above the streets of Barcelona the still unfinished Church of the Holy Family attracts thousands of visitors each year. Left is shown an ornamental lizard which stands at the entrance to the Park Guell.

MIRACLE CHILD OF MUSIC

Inside a quiet, spacious room in a tall, narrow house in Salzburg a young boy sat at his desk busily scratching with his pen on a large piece of paper. The child was completely engrossed in his task when his father and a family friend walked into the room.

"What are you writing?" the man asked his son.

"A clavier concerto," the little boy answered, "the first part is nearly finished."

His father took the paper from the boy's inky fingers and looked at the messy scrap of paper which was covered with large ink blots. At first he laughed, but then he stopped and looked closely at the notes that were written down. He stared at them for a long time and then tears of joy began to trickle down his cheeks.

At that moment Leopold Mozart realised with shattering certainty that his four-year old son was a musician of quite extraordinary talent. Six years later the whole of Europe would share his opinion of the child prodigy. At the age of ten Wolfgang Amadeus Mozart was world famous. He had given performances in all the major music centres of the world and astonished everyone who heard and saw him. But the genius who had been as a child, the wonder of all Europe, was to die neglected and penniless, buried in a pauper's grave.

The great composer was born on 27th January, 1756. His father was a musician and composer at the court of the Archbishop-Prince of the city and his book *The Violin Method* had made his name famous throughout the music world. The house

The child was completely engrossed in his task when his father and a family friend walked into the room.

in Salzburg in which Wolfgang was born was crammed with musical instruments and from the first days of his life, the child was surrounded by the atmosphere of music.

Leopold Mozart was well qualified to teach his children music and his daughter, nicknamed Nannerl, showed exceptional talent as a pianist at a very early age. When Wolfgang was four he demanded to be taught music too, and it was soon after his first lessons that he composed his clavier concerto. When he was nearly six, and his sister ten, his father decided that the time had come to show his children's remarkable talents to the world. So Leopold took them to Munich and presented them to the Bavarian prince of the city. The concert they gave at his court was a triumphant success and the Mozarts spent three exciting weeks in the city.

Leopold was so delighted with the success of the Munich visit that he and his family set out again for another trip. This time they went to Vienna, which was one of the most important centres of music in the world. There, the story of astounding success was the same.

In the June of 1763 the Mozart family set out on a Grand Tour of Europe. Everywhere they went they were treated with admiration and respect, acclaimed by kings and queens.

In London Wolfgang made friends with Johann Christian Bach, the son of the great Johann Sebastian Bach, and he soon became Wolfgang's patron and teacher. From him Mozart learned the elements of Italian opera.

It was also in London that Mozart wrote his first symphony and amazed the English court. Everyone seemed to be doubtful of his age and one Englishman sent for details of his birth from Salzburg to make sure that Mozart really was only eight years old. He found to his astonishment that the Mozarts were indeed telling the truth and all rumours about the infant prodigy's age were instantly quashed.

Before leaving England Mozart wrote six sonatas which he dedicated to Queen Charlotte and bade a sad farewell to her music master, Johann Christian Bach, the composer he was to love for the rest of his life.

Mozart did not like going home to Salzburg. Treated with great respect abroad, he and his family were virtually ignored in their native city.

His father tried to console the child and told him that soon they would be treated better by the people of Salzburg. But it took a very long time for the status of a musician to change. As Wolfgang began to grow up and was no longer a miraculous child prodigy; a spectacle to be seen and heard with wonder by the nobility, he was to face the worst kind of rudeness and condescending treatment from the ruling classes everywhere he went. Like all musicians at that time, Mozart would be treated like a humble servant, expected to dine with valets and cooks wherever he stayed.

It was not long before Europe's interest in the child musician began to fade. At the age of twelve he wrote his first opera, *The Simple Pretence*. As usual, jealous musicians had scoffed at the idea; no boy of twelve could possibly write an opera on his own, they said spitefully. But as usual, Mozart was able to silence them with the finished piece of music. All over Europe musicians were determined to make his works fail. When he went to Milan in Italy in 1769 he was offered a contract to write an opera. Jealousy caused many people to conspire against him. But despite the plots and intrigue, the

Everywhere the Mozarts went, they were treated with admiration and respect, acclaimed by kings and queens

No longer a child prodigy, Mozart was soon treated in the same way as all musicians of his time, like a humble servant, expected to dine with valets and cooks wherever he stayed.

first performance of Mozart's *Mitridate, Re di Ponto*, was a great success.

In 1777 Mozart embarked on another tour of Europe, but it was a terrible failure. As a child, he had relied greatly on the care and protection of his parents and had, in fact, been too dependant on them for his own good. Now, as a young man out in the world on his own, he suffered greatly from the loss of their presence. He had no idea how to manage his life and business affairs, could never save money, was often penniless and for the rest of his life would search for a lucrative permanent post which would make him free from financial worry. Mozart hated to be poor and wanted money to free himself from the need to beg favours of the nobility.

In 1782 he married an eighteen year old girl called Constanze Weber. The next few years brought Mozart a period of success. He started to teach music and was busy writing freelance commissions. 1786 saw the first performance of one of his greatest operas *The Marriage of Figaro*. It was an instant success and was played throughout Europe. This was followed by two other remarkable operas, *Don Giovanni* and *Cosi fan Tutte* (This Do All Women). These, too, were triumphant successes.

But despite this at the age of thirty-four Mozart was a poor man. At that time composers were paid very small sums for their works even when, as in the case of Mozart, those works were hugely successful. The best years of Mozart's life were over. He had had five children and four of them had died. He himself was often suffering illnesses, and added to the grief he felt at the loss of his children, was the heavy financial burden of a family to keep. But even when everything was going wrong for the composer, he would often have periods of joy and hope for the future. With the death of his fifth child, Mozart plunged into work, and composed his last great opera, *The Magic Flute*. Like the others, this was also well received.

In 1791 a mysterious stranger approached Mozart with a commission to write a Requiem, or Mass for the dead. The composition was, in fact, commissioned by a wealthy nobleman who intended to pass off the work as his own composition.

But while at work on the piece, Mozart fell ill, and the work was never finished. He soon realised, as he lay on his sickbed, that the work he was writing was to be his own Requiem, and by the morning of December 5th, 1791 the great composer was dead.

Haydn, another great compser, had once said. "I know that Mozart is the greatest composer living in this world." But the man who had been sadly neglected in his lifetime, was to be neglected in death too. No one followed the coffin to its final resting place in a common pauper's grave. Not even a cross was put up to mark the spot where one of the world's greatest composers was buried.

HISTORY QUIZ

Now that you have read the history section of this book, see how many of the questions you can answer in the quiz below. The answers are at the back of the book.

1. Where was the writer Jack London born?

2. In what year was the Klondike Gold Rush?

3. What is the name of the dog-hero in Jack London's book, *Call Of The Wild*?

4. What was the name of the patron for whom Rubens worked in Italy as a young man?

5. Who were the rulers of the Southern Netherlands when Rubens was alive?

6. From which monarch did Rubens receive a knighthood?

7. In what year did Rubens die?

8. What was the pseudonym of the illustrator Halbot Knight Browne?

9. Which famous children's books by Lewis Carroll did Sir John Tenniel illustrate?

10. Who wrote and illustrated *Under the Window*, *Mother Goose* and *Little Ann*?

11. Benjamin Bunny and Jemima Puddle Duck are characters created by which famous children's writer?

12. The French government commissioned Auguste Rodin to produce a series of bas reliefs. The artist was to work on this project for the rest of his life. What was this work called?

13. In 1893 Rodin was commissioned to produce a monument to one of France's greatest writers. What was this writer's name?

14. Who invented the mobile and made it into a popular art form?

15. He was born in Taragona and most of this architect's work is found in and around Barcelona. What is his name?

16. Which church did the Spanish architect have to leave unfinished at his death?

17. Where was Mozart born?

18. On a visit to London, Mozart met and became great friends of the son of a very famous composer. What was his name?

19. In 1786 one of Mozart's greatest operas was performed for the first time. What is this opera called?

20. When he died, Mozart was buried in a paupers grave. In which year did he die?

DON'T LOOK . . .

at these answers until you have tried the quizzes on pages 24, 48, 80; 104 and 128.

OUR WORLD

1. The Hopi Indians.
2. Yunnan Province. Slavery there was ended by the Communists.
3. No.
4. Sir Alan Cobham 28,000 miles.
5. A biplane.
6. The Itcha Mountains.
7. Ulgatcho.
8. Diamonds.
9. Taurepan. Mundo and Antu.
10. Five claims each of 999 acres.
11. The south geomagnetic pole.
12. Bob Thomson, a New Zealander.
13. Russia.
14. The Orkneys.
15. A necklace.
16. 1851.
17. The village of Skara Brae in the Bay of Skaill. Eight dwellings.
18. Peat.
19. They were slaves. The Communists freed them
20. Mr. A.B. Elliot.

SCIENCE

1. Pioneer 10.
2. Mars.
3. (a) Sputnik 1.
(b) Laika, a Russian dog.
(c) Explorer 1.
4. Luna III.
5. (a) Yuri Gagarin. (b) Valentina Tereshkova. Their flights began in Russia.
6. An electronic pace maker.
7. Through the nervous system.
8. To read normal type.
9. To deaden pain.
10. Protein.
11. Yeast. Oil refining.
12. Benjamin Franklin. The lightning conductor.
13. Edgar Cayce. Yes.
14. Admiral Popoff of Russia.
15. James Nasmyth. It was intended to explode when its cap hit the side of a ship.
16. He died.
17. The Eiffel Tower.
18. Telstar. Its first pictures were transmitted on 11th July, 1962.
19. A sonic torch.
20. Bagasse.